ONE NEW PEOPLE

Models for Developing a Multiethnic Church

Manuel Ortiz

InterVarsity Press
Downers Grove, Illinois

InterVarsity Press® is the book-publishing division of InterVarsity Christian Fellowship®, a student movement active on campus at hundreds of universities, colleges and schools of nursing in the United States of America, and a member movement of the International Fellowship of Evangelical Students. For information about local and regional activities, write Public Relations Dept., InterVarsity Christian Fellowship, 6400 Schroeder Rd., P.O. Box 7895, Madison, WI 53707-7895.

All Scripture quotations, unless otherwise indicated, are taken from the HOLY BIBLE, NEW INTERNATIONAL VERSION®. NIV®. Copyright © 1973, 1978, 1984 by International Bible Society. Used by permission of Zondervan Publishing House. All rights reserved.

Cover photograph: Carlos Vergara
ISBN 0-8308-1882-0

Printed in the United States of America ⊖

Library of Congress Cataloging-in-Publication Data

Ortiz, Manuel, 1938-
    One new people: models for developing a multiethnic church/by
Manuel Ortiz.
        p.   cm.
    Includes bibliographical references.
        ISBN 0-8308-1882-0
        1. Church work with minorities—United States.   2. Church and
    minorities—United States.   I. Title.
    BV4468.077   1996
    261.8'348—dc20   *96-18504*
                                                      CIP

18	17	16	15	14	13	12	11	10	9	8	7	6	5	4	3	2	1
11	10	09	08	07	06	05	04	03	02	01	00	99	98	97	96		

Dedicated to my wonderful companion
in God's vineyard
my wife Blanca

Foreword

Multiculturalism is a buzzword in contemporary society. It has affected the way we talk, the way we do politics, the way we educate, the way we see one another. Christians struggle with whether to support or attack it.

This book introduces a different sort of response to multiculturalism. You will hear very little of its echo in the secular literature. After all, churches no longer rate the front page of your daily newspaper when the world is looking for social, cultural or political solutions to their problems. However, the church has some things to teach in this area.

Nineteen hundred years ago, the church's lessons were strong enough to bring the weight of Roman society and politics tumbling down upon it and to shatter the accumulated traditions of an ancient faith. Into a world where class, power and ancestry divided rich from poor, free from slave, men from women, came a society that welcomed all who bore the name of Jesus (1 Cor 1:26-29). Into an ethnic-oriented world that isolated Jew from Greek, barbarian from Roman, came a new kind of gathering place (Gal 3:28). At the center of the gathering was the God of heaven and earth who made all flesh one and who revealed himself in the face of Jesus Christ.

These new perspectives did not come without struggle. The

church which was born out of Judaism had resisted the open-doored multiculturalism predicted by its prophets (Is 2:1-5; 60:2-3, 6; Zech 8:20-22). It took the conversion of a Roman centurion named Cornelius to help the church recall that "God has granted even to the Gentiles the repentance that leads to life" (Acts 11:18 NRSV).

Those struggles are not just past history either. Apartheid policies in the recent past of South Africa have resisted common worship and the common cup of communion. Caste traditions in India have driven untouchable from Brahmin into separate fellowships. In the United States it is still true that Sunday morning at 11 a.m. is the most segregated hour of the week. Black, white, Hispanic and Asian Christians watch each other pour out of their church buildings on street intersections that are often their only common meeting ground.

But there is another model for the church. And it is the model drawn so well by Manny Ortiz in this book—the multiethnic church. In neighborhoods in New York and Los Angeles the multiethnic church reechoes New Testament themes as diverse cultures and social classes share ministry and leadership in local congregations. And in wider geographical church structures that Presbyterians designate *presbyteries* and Baptists call *associations,* ethnically diverse congregations seek one another in a broader but visible unity.

The case studies filling the pages of this book honestly chronicle the multiethnic journey. Multiculturalism in the church is not a quick fix marked by simple tolerance for one another or by some idealistic retreat into politically correct language. Repentance for racism or ethnocentrism requires intolerance for sin; changed language is a reflection of transforming grace displayed in more than only a courtroom or public arena. Opening the doors of a church or a theological seminary to embrace cultural diversity will not be accomplished by ecclesiastical busing. It is a struggle to live out truth and justice and compassion as fellow members of the body of Christ.[1]

Two great biblical principles create the tension behind this struggle: the call to live out the unity we already possess in Christ and the celebration of that cultural diversity constantly leavened by the gospel. The church gathered at Jerusalem affirmed both principles, made visible in the work of God among the Gentiles. We belong together, they affirmed. And in that unity our cultural differences coexist (Acts 15:14, 19-20).

In a day of fear and mistrust the multiethnic church is a sample of recomposition in Christ. *E pluribus unum* is a visionary slogan in politics; in the multiethnic church it is a response of the Holy Spirit to culture wars. It is well worth more than a quick glance by a fractured society seeking unity in too many superficial solutions, and by a church that often doesn't realize the treasure it has been given. This book is an invitation to open the treasure chest of multiethnicity and rejoice.

Harvie M. Conn

1
CAPTURING
THE VISION

*F*IND A SANCTUARY ON A SUNDAY MORNING WHERE PEOPLE OF DIF-
ferent ethnic backgrounds and nationalities are worshiping together, and you will enjoy a wonderful and exciting experience, seeing
people of God from countless countries and languages call on the
name of the Lord and exalt the King of kings with all the gusto
they can muster. This experience reminds the church that Christ,
the Lord of the harvest, is greater than it can imagine, a multilingual God who understands the languages of the multitudes all
over the world. Until now we might have thought of God as siding
with our cultural group and with our concerns alone. But the
diverse group in the sanctuary reminds us that our God is also
active in other lands, caring for the child in Bangladesh and the
mother in the Tijuana countryside as well as the young man who
is selling his wares in northern Nigeria. People from all these

locales are gathered here in one place for one reason—to express their adoration to God. When the service is completed and the people begin to exit the sanctuary, profound spiritual fellowship takes place as people who have the same redeemer God engage each other. We are amazed at how wide and long and deep and high is the love of Christ that makes us members together of one body (Eph 3:18; 2:11-22).

This is what I have experienced in numerous worship and prayer services in multiethnic churches throughout the United States. The biblical themes of the sovereignty of God, the grace and love of our Christ, the all-knowing God, and the authority and universality of the Word of God were all kept in sight.

I believe that we limit the greatness of our Lord when we know God only as a local God who speaks our language and understands our conditions alone. The multiethnic church provides us with a more comprehensive understanding of the Scriptures. It takes away our haughtiness—our belief that we are more important and more knowledgeable than anyone else. It teaches us to learn the Word in more depth because the insights of others help us to see things that our blinders shut out before. It tells us that we need each other (1 Cor 12:12-27) and that one part cannot tell another, "I have no need of you." The Great Commission is expressed through the testimonies of individuals with many accents and translations saying that their salvation is bought by the One we affectionately call Jesus.

This is our world. We are not of one kind, we are of many; yet we have the same God and the same unchanging Scriptures. This multiethnic phenomenon is becoming the norm of every society. To try to hide from the growing multiethnicity will not do. Our children and their children will have to learn what we have not taught them—to love God and others who are different from ourselves and to live in unity in the reality of diversity. The kingdom of God and the lasting work of the church are not served by contemporary Jonahs who balk until they eventually submit and learn what the sovereign Lord has prepared for us.

This book has been written to address the concerns of a changing world. We need to accept the challenge of mission, rather than seeking to withdraw or to escape. The gospel is our comfort and our strength; it is radical, and it will demonstrate that it is the power of God to salvation to all who believe (Rom 1:16).

I grew up in the fascinating city of New York. In the borough of Manhattan I was introduced to a multiethnic community in which people had to depend on each other in spite of their differences. The immigrant groups that were arriving through Ellis Island had not yet polarized, and the freshness of new beginnings as well as the vulnerability of new entrants humbled people and caused them to look to anyone for assistance.

This community on 112th Street was filled with commotion, ethnic diversity, languages that were strange to all of us, and wonderful aromas that teased our senses while our parents cooked our evening meals. I learned several languages by necessity in order to speak to the parents of my friends. Housing projects had not yet segregated our communities, and in our ignorance and our vulnerability we learned to make a diverse community work. As time went on, community boundaries were established, and turf wars became the norm in the streets of Manhattan. It was now Little Italy, El Barrio (Spanish Harlem) and Harlem where many if not most of the African-Americans lived. Eventually the schools were also segregated. The whole process intensified as time went on. But I continue to cherish memories of that wonderful period during my youth when struggling people needed each other and people honored their common humanity.

When I became a Christian, I recognized that the world had infiltrated the church and that the life of the church was in most cases segregated, by design and by desire, on the basis of racism and ethnocentrism. By this time we were no longer as vulnerable as we had been in the initial stages of our immigration into this country. By now we had learned that some cultures were good, while others were not beneficial. The church did more than meet together because of similarities; it practiced exclusion toward those who were dissimilar.

How This Book Came to Be Written

In 1994 I was awarded a research grant by the Association of Theological Schools to study the multiethnic church in the United States with the goal of helping the church wrestle with issues of multiethnicity in the context of local ministries. In order to achieve this, I developed a multifaceted research strategy. The first phase was gathering general background material and identifying multiethnic churches for in-depth case study analysis. This phase included (1) sending questionnaires to 201 denominational executives and mission personnel, seminary professors teaching practical theology and missions, and personal contacts, asking for their definitions of multiethnic ministry and seeking their recommendations of possible multiethnic models to further investigate; (2) doing a demographic analysis of current immigration flows, their composition and their destinations using the 1990 census as well as sociological studies, and (3) locating published and unpublished literature that tackles multiethnic church issues, primarily focusing on missions and local church case studies. From this material

I was able to select ten churches representing both multiethnic and multicongregational models from across the country in areas with varying immigration influence. I used three approaches in evaluating these churches: (1) direct on-site interaction and examination, (2) phone and on-site interviews, and (3) gathering literature that pertained to the particular church being evaluated. These church evaluations formed the basis of the model approach used in this book.

As I visited churches on the East Coast, churches on the West Coast and churches in numerous cities in between, I was pleasantly surprised to find the church growing in this pluralistic milieu without compromising the gospel of Jesus Christ. I found the church not only attempting to meet the needs of the multitudes but also finding joy in a gospel that was plainly presented and was transforming people into a new humanity bought in Christ. The Lord is gathering the masses to himself, no matter what their religious backgrounds or cultural traditions. The church is reaping the harvest and rejoicing in worship of this trinitarian God who desires the worship of all people.

I am grateful to ATS and Westminster Theological Seminary for the opportunity to do this study and to complete a work that has set me on yet another course of study: the development of multiethnic small groups and multiethnic church planting methods in the urban context. I am also deeply appreciative to my family, particularly my wife, Blanca, for their patience and involvement in this study. Sue Baker, a friend and coworker in ministry for many years, provided the avenue for in-depth research and consultation as we visited churches and reviewed immigration patterns. Harvie Conn continues to be an inspiration to me in the matter of writing and research, especially as it refers to the missiological development of urban ministry. I am also grateful to all the pastors and church leaders who took time to meet with me in the midst of their heavy schedules, filling out questionnaires and dialoguing with me regarding the issues I was discovering, and to Julie Faust, a friend and a constant reminder of God's grace.

Use of Models

Church models are used extensively in some chapters to demonstrate how principles are fleshed out in a practical sense. As you read these models, you will be tempted to apply aspects of them immediately because they seem successful, dynamic and similar to your present situation (or because you may be simply desperate for help). But this can be dangerous if you do not give careful consideration to certain principles.

James Spradley provides assistance in our move toward exegesis. He states that "every social situation can be identified by three primary elements: *a place, actors, and activities.*"[1] The multiethnic church is both a spiritual dynamic that is founded on biblical teaching and a social reality that has interactive components where people from a unique social and cultural context come together. Therefore, the social realities are important and must not be ignored if we are to engage people with integrity. I have altered the terms used by Spradley in order to fit our frame of thinking. I will use *context, people* and *actions.* In some cases the models have been examined from only one or two angles. Usually the people and the actions are the aspects evaluated. But this does not provide the reader with the full picture and may be misleading. All three aspects need to be reviewed in order to understand how each model functions.

The *context* primarily involves the local geographical situation that defines where people are living and who is leaving and entering the community. The model is often dependent on this kind of information because it indicates that a church may have become multiethnic because of a major transition in its community and the arrival of many new ethnic groups. The base of operation could be parish ministry that focused on the context, which through community analysis indicated the time was prime to do crosscultural ministries. The leaving group might have been the long-standing group that had lived in that community for many years and made up a major segment of the church. Evaluating the local trends of people leaving and entering will be important to doing multiethnic ministry.

Understanding the context also has to do with national trends of migration. In the next chapter we will identify the major receiving cities that serve as ports of entry for new migrants. Los Angeles is one of these cities, so we would expect to find numerous churches there moving toward multiethnicity as well as various denominations that are successfully utilizing this migration flow for the furtherance of the gospel ministry. Often the context determines the viability of the ministry and possibly its long-range effect. Models, therefore, have to be read from their context.

The second aspect is *people*. In this case the model is best understood in terms of the makeup of the people who live in the community, including their worldview, cultural values and religious beliefs. Who are the people in the community? And who are the people in the church? Both must be studied. Very often the community is undergoing rapid ethnic change, but the congregation in the church may not be ready to engage its new neighbors. It is important to have some way of doing an ethnographic study in the community as well as in the church. James Spradley notes that ethnography

> reveals what people think and shows us the cultural meanings they use daily. It is the one systematic approach in the social sciences that leads us into those separate realities which others have learned and which they use to make sense out of their worlds. In our complex society the need for understanding how other people see their experience has never been greater. Ethnography is a tool with great promise: It offers the educator a way of seeing schools through the eyes of the students. . . . Ethnography offers all of us the chance to step outside our narrow cultural backgrounds, to set aside our socially inherited ethnocentrism, if only for a brief period, and to apprehend the world from the viewpoint of other human beings who live by different meaning systems.[2]

This approach allowed me to observe the multiethnic church through the eyes of those participating in it and to document what they, the church leaders and members, are doing and how they are proceeding with what they understand to be the work of the sovereign Lord in carrying out the Great Commission in the United States. It is important to note that in every city there is a certain ethos, a distinguishing characteristic, that influences the church and its ministry. The Hispanics of Chicago may be different in various aspects from the Hispanics in either New York or Los Angeles. This will also influence how ministry is done.

The third aspect is *actions.* This primarily deals with how the groups interact with each other—lines of communication, leadership involvement, and ownership of the church and its ministries. I have discovered that what may seem to be multiethnic from the outside might not prove to be truly multiethnic when viewed from the inside.

You should pay attention to the different histories of the churches represented in our models. The history and makeup of each church provides a unique dynamic for developing a particular multiethnic congregation. Also pay attention to the leaders guiding the church in order to identify their gifts and experiences in ministry. You should not try to copy something that is uniquely displayed in a particular leader or pastor unless it is appropriate to your context.

It is important to learn to use the social sciences and to read models for the benefit of the Lord's kingdom. Too often we read models of ministry without sufficient critical reflection. We need new and effective models, but it is wrong to assume that a model that works for one church will also work for us. Contextualization dimensions must be scrutinized in order to see if they belong in a different context.

Overview of Chapters

The chapters that follow are sequenced to assist concerned Christians in understanding the multiethnic development of the local church and to encourage them to participate in the ongoing mission of reaching and discipling those who already live in our communities, as well as those arriving from other countries, with the holistic gospel of Jesus Christ.

Chapter two, "Who Is My Neighbor?" attempts to open our understanding of population and immigrant groups. It is important to read this chapter with an open mind to discover the great opportunities that are available to you. Do not get bogged down with the data; be patient with information because it will help you to prepare your heart and your mind for the chapters to come. As you read, you should ask yourself several questions. First, who are the people near my community? How many of them are living in the city closest to my church? What cities are receiving most of the immigrants, and how should I pray for the churches in that area? What are the characteristics of the incoming groups in regard to, say, income, education and age?

Chapter three discusses the purpose of multiethnic church development. Actual models are presented as examples of various biblical themes that provide a rationale for a commitment to multiethnic ministry. In this chapter you will learn how, in general, multiethnic churches are formed. In most cases they originate in a biblical commitment.

You should ask yourself, What are my commitments in pursuing the development of a multiethnic church? How do I fit into one of the paradigms listed? Is my church carrying out the mandate I see in some of the models listed in this chapter? Am I encouraged as I read about these actual models? How can I pray for them as I see the potential for great outreach in the cities of this country? At this point you should be feeling more comfortable with the language of multiethnicity and with the possibility of seeing this kind of ministry become a reality in your context and church.

Now you are ready to review multicongregational (chapter four) and multiethnic (chapter five) models. Multicongregational and multiethnic church models follow different principles. Chapters four and five provide models of each of these types, highlighting aspects that are different from each other. The following five questions may be useful for you to keep in mind as we go through the models. You may want to jot down questions that occur to you as your study proceeds.

1. How is the multiethnic church defined? What is a multicongregational church? What is a multiethnic church? Some may

say that a multiethnic church (MEC) is a church that houses various ethnic groups from the community in one building with different meeting times during the week. This is what we call a multicongregational church. Others may say a church has to have a certain percentage of different cultural groups for it to qualify as an MEC, for example, a church that has 60 percent white, 20 percent black and 20 percent Hispanic congregants. Still others may consider an MEC as one in which all ethnic groups meet together for worship at the same time and utilize different languages (with the assistance of translation). There are many other possibilities. The subject of definition is one that continues to come up in most discussions of multiethnicity. Just as a church that is considered homogeneous must have one culture that permeates all aspects of the ministry, from leadership to worship styles and congregational makeup, a heterogeneous church must have multiethnicity permeating all of the ministry of the church. Many pastors are concerned that multiethnicity not become something to grow the church numerically without resolving the intense conflict caused by injustice and racial alienation in the church and in society.

2. Once created, how do multiethnic churches avoid reverting to homogeneity?

3. What theological similarities and dissimilarities exist among multiethnic churches?

4. What influence does the community have on the establishment of the multiethnic church? And how does the church influence the community?

5. What implications does the multiethnic church hold for race reconciliation and justice?

As we move into chapter four, "Multicongregational Church

Models," you will finally be able to clear up the subject of definition—what is a multicongregational church and how does it function? This chapter provides models of successful crosscultural ministries that seem to be having a great deal of fun and excitement
in the process. You will glean principles from this chapter that will
help you establish or encourage the formation of a multicongregational church. Ask yourself several questions. Are all three categories—the renting model, the celebration model and the integrative model—possible for effective ministry in my community and
church? Do I see more possibilities in any one of these models? If
so, which one and why? What other principles can I add to this
list? The final question in this chapter is, What have I learned from
these models and grasped experientially? This chapter should give
you a more profound understanding of the multiethnic dynamic.
You should not feel overwhelmed with all that is accomplished in
these ministries. Rather, you should believe that the Lord led many
of these men and women in the creative expressions of God's kingdom in a pluralistic society, just as God has done in the past.

Chapter four also raises the issue of race and ethnic reconciliation. How do you stand on this subject from a personal/experien-
tial and a biblical framework? How do you feel when you are with
people who are culturally different from you? What is racism? Is
it something that can occur in a church that claims the authority
of the Word of God and the lordship of Christ?

Chapter five leads us into what is often challenged by many (in
their reactive speech) as the church that "will never work." The
multiethnic church provides us with a window into the coming
kingdom of God, where diverse groups will be gathered in one
place, singing praises to the Lord in the end times. All these people
of God will be as one forever and ever, wearing the white robes that

symbolize their righteousness in Christ. In this chapter you should ask yourself questions that were raised in chapter four and then exegete the models. Make up your own list of principles to see if we are in line with each other.

At this point you may want to assess critically both the multi-congregational and the multiethnic church models. This is a good time to evaluate your understanding of this subject and to take note of what you have learned. Write out the principles for establishing a multiethnic or a multicongregational church before reading chapter six. If you note leadership qualities in your list, you are moving in the right direction, and you will find this exercise very important to your personal development. By now you should have read critically the material provided, and you should be coming to some conclusions in your thinking concerning crosscultural ministry. This is good development for leadership in a multiethnic setting. Now read the list I have provided for leadership development and see how much we differ. You may have much to offer in the process of doing this kind of ministry, and some of your points may be more relevant than the ones I have provided. Remember, we are all learners who are changing and growing in the process.

Chapter seven is meant to help us wrestle with the process of transition. Transitions are normal to everything that is alive. Life itself is a constant procession of transitions. The church must be prepared for changes. What transitions have you experienced in life? How have you received them? Can some of the transitions listed in this chapter be profitable for God's kingdom? Which ones? I use a key word, *intentionality*. What does it mean to you as you read through some of the steps described in this chapter? At this point we have gone from looking at models and understanding some of the dynamics to attempting to work through some actual issues that the church will face. Pray about your commitment and about the implementation of these principles.

Now that we have achieved some understanding of the theory of the multiethnic/multicongregational church, you will want to read chapter eight for a discussion of why this work is necessary. The goal of the multiethnic church is to urge the body of Christ, in all its diversity, to be Christian, as described in the Bible. The biblical material and the practical principles will help you work out this calling. Ask yourself if your goal is also to see a new humanity, growing in Christ and transcending culture.

Chapter nine is the final, but not necessarily the concluding, chapter. It reminds me of the last chapter in the book of Acts, which leaves the impression that there is more to come. That continuation involves doing, implementing and utilizing the suggestions in what I call "homework." We have a missiological task ahead of us, and we have by now realized the essential tools for doing this task. Have you found the content of this book inspiring or tiring? I hope that you are feeling inspired.

The study questions for small group discussion at the end of each chapter are intended to enhance the process of this wonderful opportunity of serving the Lord within a diverse community and congregation.

A Final Word

The world is coming not only into our geographical boundaries but also into our total life experience. We are learning how to meet new people without stumbling with our body language. We are by necessity learning how to twist our tongues in a new manner in order to pronounce unfamiliar names. Because immigration from

Asia, Africa and Latin America is highly visible, we are beginning to get in touch with our own roots in order to answer the question, Where do we come from? God is declaring to us a new means of mission that is really an old means of mission based on the incarnation of Christ that we go and make disciples of all nations (Mt 28:19). We will not have to go very far, only a short walk down the street.

All of life is based on relationships, beginning with our God, who desires fellowship with his children, and moving into our families, communities and churches. In all of this we recognize the necessity of meeting with people and of sharing in the joys and sorrows that these relationships bring. In this engagement we discern that crossing gender, ethnic and racial lines sometimes brings a certain amount of conflict and discomfort. Here in the United States, as well as in many other countries, the globalization process is bringing the world into our neighborhoods and communities, and relationship-building in biblical terms is greatly in demand. Christ calls us to love our neighbor (Mt 19:19) and to love strangers and the unprotected (Heb 13:1-3).

Racism continues to get headline attention in the daily news. It is an illness that seems to be contagious. It has come to permeate our institutions as well as the individual on the street. The church cannot be excluded from this charge; on the contrary, criticism is pinned heavily on the church in general, and on the evangelical church in particular. There is a need for us to review our present personal and corporate status in reference to racial conflict and biblical integrity.

The church should take the leadership in these matters of justice and reconciliation. In some cases we have failed to do so and have added to the problem rather than providing a solution. This display of apathy is in need of correction. As the world continues to find its "home" here in the United States, we are being challenged by the sovereign God to practice the love and justice of our Lord in a multiethnic society. The gospel of glory is transformational and can bring holistic healing to both sides of the cultural spectrum.

2
WHO IS
MY NEIGHBOR?

I HAVE LIVED IN SEVERAL LARGE CITIES—NEW YORK, CHICAGO AND Philadelphia. It is clear to me that we are living in a world-village of many people and many cultures. The world is stepping into our living room in what seems to be a permanent move. Immigrants are not coming to visit or to obtain a college education, but to make this country their home without altering their cultural norms.

When I, as a Puerto Rican, wake up to the hustle and bustle of the African-American community in which I live, I realize that there are similarities and dissimilarities in our lifestyles, yet we live as neighbors. When I go to our favorite grocery store to buy the ingredients to make our regular Puerto Rican meals, I discern that the owners are from an area not associated with Latin America—

they are Palestinian. I go to the cobbler shop, and the man who tells me that my shoes will be ready by five o'clock is from Southeast Asia. The hardware store is close by, and I walk over to have an additional set of keys made. The owner speaks to me of her home in Seoul, Korea, in a tone suggesting that she would like to be there for the summer months.

This quick one-hour tour of my community illustrates my understanding that we are not living in a U.S.A. of the 1960s, but rather in one that is unfamiliar to many of us. An article by Barbara Vobejda in the *Philadelphia Inquirer* tells us that "the United States has the largest foreign-born population in its history. . . . Nearly 32 million people speak a language other than English at home."[1] Jerry Appleby, in his very handy book *Missions Have Come to America,* lists numerous findings that cannot be ignored. "The United States has the second-largest Black population of any country in the world (Nigeria is first). . . . America has the fourth-largest Spanish population in the world."[2]

The world is in a state of movement, responding to what demographers call push-pull factors, and it is making its mark on America. We must welcome our new residents with love and compassion. In 1985 *Time* magazine entitled an issue " 'The Changing Face of America': How Long Will It Be Before the Third World Overwhelms the First World?"[3] In 1990 there appeared an issue entitled "What Will the U.S. Be Like When Whites Are No Longer the Majority?"[4] These titles and their accompanying articles impress on us that the "new immigration" is drastically changing the look of many of our communities and challenging our perception of who is "American."

Who is our neighbor, and how shall we be neighbors in the name of Christ? Few are asking this question, in my opinion, because of fear of the unknown and also because of the ongoing racism that afflicts this country.

The New Immigration

By the year 2000 more than 50 percent of college-aged young people in America will be people of color. California is undergoing such a radical transformation that within fifteen years 50 percent of the state will be made up of people of color. This process is also taking place in Florida, New York and Texas. It is striking to note that Los Angeles has been referred to as the "immigrant capital of the world."[5]

In order to assess the multiethnic situation in the United States, we need demographic information that we can utilize to formulate strategies for outreach. The immigration policies that are currently in place indicate how the future will stack up in reference to local church ministries.

Initially, there was no immigration policy in the United States. Anybody who managed to make it to the "New World" could enter. The first attempt at regulating the flow of immigration occurred with the Immigration Act of 1882 that set up qualitative standards aimed at excluding undesirables—criminals, mental incompetents, the seriously ill and Asians. In 1924 the nature of restrictions was changed from qualitative to quantitative, and a quota system was established. This act was aimed at freezing the ethnic balance of the country. It did so by restricting groups that did not already have a stronghold in the United States. The main, but not the only, ethnic target was Japan. The first philosophical change in immigration policy came with the Immigration Act of 1965. This law "repealed the national origins quotas and restrictions against Asians and substituted a preference system based upon family unification, occupations, and refugee status."[6] This new act caused a major change in the composition of the U.S. immigrant flow. Robert Pastor points out that "between 1900 and 1965, 75 percent of all immigrants were of European extraction."[7] Because of the new immigration policy, however, by 1978 82 percent of immigrants were coming from Asia and Latin America.[8]

Population groups in the United States are primarily categorized through use of the census racial breakdown. Currently the U.S. census recognizes five racial categories: White; Black; American Indian, Eskimo and Aleut; Asian and Pacific Islander; and Other. Hispanics are actually made up of a number of races (e.g., American Indian through indigenous native groups, black through the introduction of slaves, and white through Spanish colonizers) and are not considered a race. However, we can identify Hispanics of the various races, which allows us to manipulate the census figures, and we can come up with White, Black, Asian, Hispanic and Other as racial/ethnic categories that will be helpful throughout the following analysis. Figure 1 shows the U.S. population in 1990 by our new categories.

Although whites still maintain a clear majority, making up 76 percent of the U.S. population, other racial and ethnic groups have great numerical significance in specific parts of the country. All groups except "Other" are highly represented in metropolitan areas. However, blacks, Asians and Hispanics are much more apt to be living in central cities. Therefore, the church must view our central cities with a multiethnic missional objective.

Our city populations are not constant. Much has been written about white flight, which has resulted in many of our major central cities being occupied by blacks and new immigrant groups. The major migration of southern blacks to northern cities has ended.

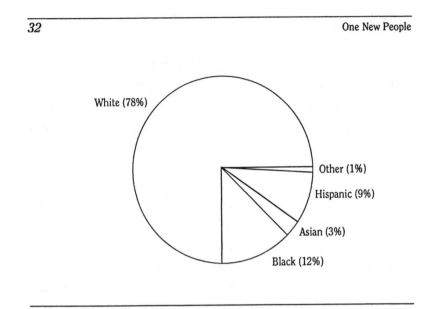

Figure 1. U.S. Population by Race/Ethnicity, 1990.
Source: 1990 U.S. Census STF-1C CD-ROM data file.

Many of our cities are actually declining in total population, yet there is still one major source of population increase in the cities—immigrants—and these newcomers are changing the face of many urban areas. Exactly who are they? Where do they come from? Where are they settling in the United States?

Who Are the "Recent Immigrants"?
Before we discuss who makes up recent immigrant groups, we must take note of one group that technically does not fall into this category—Puerto Ricans. As a U.S. commonwealth, Puerto Rico is considered part of the country, and Puerto Ricans are U.S. citizens. Their movement to the U.S. mainland is considered much the same as movement from Pennsylvania to Illinois, for example. Culturally Puerto Ricans resemble other Hispanic immigrant groups (both in terms of their own needs and in terms of their adaptation to a

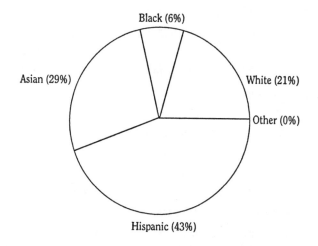

Figure 2. Race/Ethnicity of New Arrivals to the U.S., 1985-1990.
Source: 1990 U.S. Census One-Percent Public Use Microdata Sample.

majority Anglo, Eurocentric culture) much more than they do U.S. interstate movers. As we try to identify those groups confronting the U.S. church with the challenge of multiethnicity, we must include Puerto Ricans along with the other Hispanics.

The U.S. census identifies those who lived outside the United States in 1985 but were residents in 1990. If we eliminate those born in the U.S. (representing U.S. citizens living abroad) and add those living in Puerto Rico in 1985, we can come up with a measure of new arrivals to the United States. Figure 2 shows that 43 percent of these new arrivals were Hispanic and 29 percent were Asian. Therefore, we will concentrate our analysis on these two groups.

Age/Gender Changes Among New Arrivals
Overall, as would be expected, the immigrant groups are quite young. However, as the following age pyramids (figure 3) indicate,

Hispanics are much more concentrated in the "under 30" age brackets (53.2 percent of Asian men and 51.4 percent of Asian women are under age 30, whereas 69.7 percent of Hispanic men and 64.0 percent of Hispanic women are this young). Since our method of determining recent arrivals is based on residence in 1985 of all those enumerated in the 1990 census, obviously all children under the age of five are not counted (as they had no residence in 1985). This means that the age groups are even younger than the figures show.

As Reimers points out, the traditional immigrant of the past was a male in his prime working years. Since 1930, however, a slight majority of immigrants have been women.[9] When we look at our two major recent arrival groups, we notice that there are more Asian women than men (615,000 to 579,000, respectively). Hispanics present a more traditional pattern, with 950,000 men and 815,000 women.

As church programs are often based on age or gender categories, it is important to recognize the different set of needs Asians and Hispanics will present to a church. Asians tend to be coming as families to make a new life in the United States. But Hispanics, especially Puerto Ricans and Mexicans, are following the older immigration pattern of sending young men to earn money to send home so that they can return to their homeland. This produces a cyclical, transitional group of young men going and coming in response to economic pressures faced by their extended families in their homeland.

Educational Differences Among New Arrivals

Besides age and gender differences between our Asian and Hispanic recent arrivals, educational differences can be a very important

Asian Age Pyramid

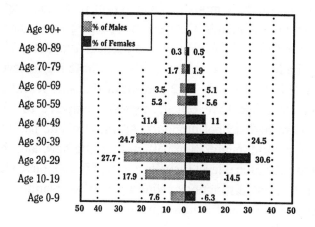

Hispanic Age Pyramid

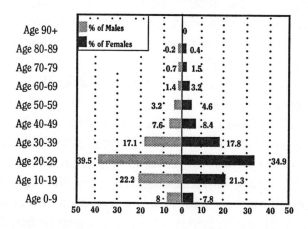

Figure 3. Age Pyramids for Asian and Hispanic Recent Immigrants, 1985-1990.
Source: 1990 U.S. Census One-Percent Public Use Microdata Sample.

consideration when devising strategies for incorporating the groups into a multiethnic ministry. Asian recent immigrants aged twenty-five and older include 41.4 percent college graduates and, at the other extreme, 25.0 percent high-school dropouts. This agrees with the findings that recent immigrants have higher levels of education.[10] However, only 12.2 percent of Hispanic recent arrivals of the same age have college degrees, compared to 57.3 percent who are high-school dropouts. Again, Hispanic patterns are more like the old immigration pattern than the new, and this differential in educational level (usually mirrored in economic status) will create class distinctions requiring creative planning in order to have a unified multiethnic ministry.

Where Are the Recent Immigrants?

Recent immigrants have not settled evenly across the country. Waldinger found that the "recent arrivals are overwhelmingly to be found in metropolitan areas, where they live, to a disproportionate extent, in central cities; the newcomers are even more overrepresented in the ten principal receiving areas."[11]

In 1980 these receiving areas included Los Angeles, New York, Miami, Chicago, San Francisco, Washington, D.C., Anaheim, Houston, San Diego and Boston.[12] Our own analysis of 1990 data shows that a full 74 percent of recent immigrants (not including new arrivals from Puerto Rico) settled in only seven states: California, Florida, Illinois, Massachusetts, New Jersey, New York and Texas. Puerto Ricans have traditionally settled in the Northeast, but the state receiving the largest number of new arrivals from the island was Florida (20.9 percent). New York, historically the settlement place of choice, received only 18.6 percent, followed by Massachusetts with 10.9 percent and New Jersey with 9.8 percent.

Local Differences Among Immigrant Populations

All of the figures above indicate that the nature of the multiethnic church will be quite different, depending on the local context. As New York and Los Angeles are the two largest immigrant receiving areas, we will compare a number of immigrant characteristics for these two metropolitan areas in order to gain a sense of the necessity of exegeting the local context before developing ministries. Up to this point, we have lumped people from many nations into the categories of Asian and Hispanic. As we review issues in Los Angeles and New York, you should not only look at differences between Asians and Hispanics but also look at differences based on national origin within these groups.

Generational/Language Issues

One major consideration in developing multiethnic ministries is language. There is one set of crosscultural dynamics that is operative when bringing together various groups that all speak English. There is a different set of dynamics working when numerous languages are represented. Within these sets of differences we also find crossgenerational differences, first-generation immigrants being much more protective of the traditions and customs of their homeland. Therefore, it is important for us to determine the nativity of our different groups as well as their English language proficiency.

In the Los Angeles metropolitan area 66.3 percent of the entire population is native-born, but this figure is much lower among Asians (28.1 percent) and Hispanics (45.4 percent). If we split the Asian and Hispanic populations into national origin groups, we find seven Asian and ten Hispanic groups with at least twenty thousand residents in the area. Of the individual Asian groups, only the Japanese have a high percentage of native-born (67.2 percent). All the other major Asian groups are much newer, with the majority arriving in the U.S. since 1970. The Hispanic national groups are a little more diverse, with over half of the Spaniards, Mexicans and Puerto Ricans being born in the U.S., the Cubans and Ecuadorans steadily arriving since 1960, and the other groups primarily arriving since 1980.

In the Los Angeles metropolitan area fifty-eight languages other than English were identified by the census sample. Of these, four—Spanish, Chinese (Cantonese), Korean and Tagalog (Filipino)—are spoken by over one hundred thousand people, with close to two and a half million speaking Spanish. Regardless of primary language spoken, proficiency in English is diverse. Filipinos and Asian Indians are fairly proficient in English, but over 30 percent of all other Asian groups do not speak English "well" or "very well." None of the Spanish groups are as proficient in English as the Filipinos and Asian Indians, but the percentage of those with English-speaking problems range from 13.8 (for Spaniards) to 46.7 (for Guatemalans). Overall, over one-third of Hispanics have problems with English. Obviously multilingual congregations and ministries will be necessary in many parts of the area, and English-speaking congregations could be quite diverse culturally as they service the second generation and beyond of these different national groups.

The New York metropolitan area's Asian population represents five national origin groups with a population of at least twenty thousand, while there are eleven major Hispanic national origin groups. The Asian population has 80.6 percent foreign-born and is quite new, with the majority of all groups arriving since 1970. As in Los Angeles, the Hispanic groups are more diverse than the

Asian groups. Over half of the Spaniards and Puerto Ricans were born in the United States, Cubans and Panamanians have been arriving steadily since 1960, and the other groups have come since 1970. Forty-four languages are spoken in New York, but only Chinese (Cantonese) with 204,000, and Spanish, with almost a million and a half, present extensive language use. As in Los Angeles, the Filipinos and Asian Indians are quite proficient in English, but the other Asian groups have problems, ranging from 25.1 percent of Japanese to 44.3 percent of Chinese. Spaniards, Puerto Ricans and Panamanians all have less than 20 percent with English difficulties, but the other groups have much more difficulty, with Mexicans having the most problems. Again, multiethnic churches will have to deal with multilingual congregations or ministries.

Socioeconomic Characteristics

Many urban pastors attempting multiethnic ministries comment that crossing socioeconomic barriers can be even more difficult than crossing racial or ethnic lines. Therefore, it would be helpful to examine differences in socioeconomic indicators between national groups in our metropolitan areas. One way to compare the socioeconomic levels of various groups is to compare the percentage of those groups that are middle class or better (with incomes at least twice that of the official poverty level) with the percentage in poverty (at or below the poverty level). A second way to look at the overall economic well-being of a group is to compare median family incomes.[13]

In Los Angeles we notice large economic differences within our two major immigrant ethnic groups, depending on national origin. Over two-thirds of the Asians are middle class or higher; in fact, more than three-fourths of the Filipinos, Japanese and Asian Indians are middle class or higher. Cambodians are much poorer than the other groups, with 43.2 percent living in poverty. Hispanics do not exhibit the same extremes. Overall, 44.8 percent are middle class, but only Spaniards have over three-fourths in that category. Guatemalans and Nicaraguans have the most in poverty, 30.6 and 33.5 percent respectively.

Table 1 looks at median family incomes for each of the major Asian and Hispanic groups in Los Angeles. Overall, Asian incomes appear to be much higher than Hispanic incomes, but there is tremendous variation in both groups as we look at national origin. These differences reflect a number of factors, including educational attainment, newness in the U.S., and issues of discrimination (the reception that the host people extends to the individual groups).

Table 1. Median Family Incomes for Los Angeles Asian and Hispanic National Origin Groups with over 20,000 Population, 1990.

Asian		Hispanic	
Asian Indian	$42,600	Ecuadorian	$37,456
Japanese	42,000	Spaniard	36,000
Filipino	41,300	Peruvian	27,000
Chinese	36,500	Cuban	26,683
Vietnamese	28,641	Puerto Rican	25,500
Korean	25,000	Mexican	25,028
Cambodian	16,656	Nicaraguan	21,000
		Honduran	19,300
		Salvadoran	19,250
		Guatemalan	18,000

Source: 1990 U.S. Census One-Percent Public Use Microdata Sample.

The contrast is even more stark in New York, where over 50 percent of all Asian groups were middle class or better, but only six of the eleven Hispanic groups reached that level. Two of the Hispanic groups—Puerto Ricans and Dominicans—had over one-third of their people living in poverty. Median incomes are shown in table 2. In New York we find large ranges among both Asians and Hispanics; however, Hispanics again seem to be lower.

Table 2. Median Incomes for New York Asian and Hispanic National Origin Groups with over 20,000 Population, 1990.

Asian		Hispanic	
Filipino	$40,000	Spaniard	$38,000
Japanese	38,700	Cuban	27,258
Asian Indian	35,749	Panamanian	24,163
Chinese	27,505	Peruvian	24,002
Korean	24,400	Colombian	22,354
		Ecuadorian	21,600
		Mexican	21,417
		Honduran	20,000
		Salvadoran	19,500
		Dominican	16,000
		Puerto Rican	16,000

Source: 1990 U.S. Census One-Percent Public Use Microdata Sample.

In a society like the U.S. that assigns great value to being a "success," economic differences can lead to feelings of superiority or inferiority. It is especially crucial in a multiethnic ministry to assert a biblical system of ascribing value (to individuals or to groups) on the basis of the fact that all of us are unique creations of God and bear his image rather than on the basis of a societal stratification system. Otherwise, reconciliation between groups will be extremely difficult.

Conclusion

This demographic analysis was placed at the beginning of the book to assist those who are pursuing multiethnic ministries by motivating them to continue to do their homework as they establish congregations within an ethnically diverse community. Many of these new groups pose language barriers that have to be taken into consideration when devising a strategy. Differing levels of education have led to economic diversity both within and between the national origin groups. Thus, strategies must account for reconciliation between socioeconomic levels as well as racial and ethnic groups. All of these variations are displayed in different patterns that depend on the local context.

We live in a racist and ethnocentric society that wants us to ignore our neighbors, especially if they are different from us, and to believe that in some way or another that our culture is superior. At the present time in our history we are asking the question, How do we come together as diverse people in a manner that honors the Lord and his Word? The homogeneous unit principle (HUP) has been the paradigm for missions and church planting for so long that it is difficult for Christian institutions, Christian colleges and seminaries to get away from it. But some are trying to understand their future in relation to immigration and globalization heterogeneously and without compromising the gospel. In some cases the church is aware of its shortcomings and wants to know what to do about them. Can the church in the U.S. be a model of reconciliation? This is our mission—to grow both qualitatively and quantitatively in a multiethnic milieu.

Small Group Discussion Questions

1. This chapter speaks quite candidly about societal change. What do you observe in your local community, workplace or place of recreation that has undergone change, particularly ethnic change?

2. What feelings overcome you as you observe these changes? Share them as honestly as you can.

3. The Great Commission is a biblical text that is often used in reference to reaching out to the multitudes, especially those who are ethnically different from us. How can you obey the command in Matthew 28:19-20? What are some practical ways in which you are able to understand and participate in the Great Commission?

4. In reference to your church community, how can you make your friends more aware of the changes that are going on in the world and of the mission opportunities that God has provided for you?

3

THE PURPOSE
OF MULTIETHNIC
CHURCH
DEVELOPMENT

---

*M*Y JOURNEY INTO RESEARCHING THE MULTIETHNIC CHURCH IN
the United States was an eye opener that conjured up in me a
renewed commitment to the church as well as a sense of responsibility to continue this research. As I maneuvered into this project, I also discovered that many of my assumptions needed revi-
sion. Definitions on which I had depended for direction and
meaning needed reflection and discussion in order for me to better
understand the subject.

Peter Wagner says that we have multiethnic churches for the

purpose of evangelism and church growth. His concern is that people are served best in their own cultural and linguistic milieu. He suggests that the homogeneous unit principle (HUP) espoused by church growth folks at the Fuller School of World Mission is the only way to go in growing a church in the context of ethnic minorities or of any community, for that matter. This principle asserts that churches grow better if the congregants come from the same background (particularly ethnic and socioeconomic). I agree with some of this thinking but have reservations as to its being the only way. My research suggests that the intentional attempts by local ministries to create multiethnic and multicongregational churches that have been most productive are the ones that move toward reconciliation.

Wagner believes that the HUP will in no way promote segregated and racist churches.[1] I disagree with his conclusions. I believe HUP has been a hindrance to race relations and to racial and ethnic reconciliation in the Christian community. At this time we, the church in the U.S., are a great disappointment in terms of manifesting the new community founded in Christ Jesus and called to worship the King of the kingdom in the ministry of reconciliation. Where the context has called us to mirror the gospel of the kingdom in this world of ever increasing diversity, we must take care to be obedient. This is provided by the multiethnic church, a church that reflects the unity of the Godhead, one that introduces the good news to a world that has come to understand hostility and division as the norm. Reconciliation becomes the top priority of the MEC.

The MEC may grow and have success numerically, but if it has not worked through the issues of division and hostility that have long separated the church, it falls short of being a multiethnic church, in my opinion. We live in a disturbed society in which we want to ignore neighbors who are different. We may even work against their ever becoming our neighbors.

As I spoke with pastors and church leaders, I realized that there were several biblical passages that moved churches into a multiethnic dynamic. The question is whether or not their conclusions are sufficient. The following are biblical themes that display this concern along with church models that exemplify each theme.

The Matthew 28:16-20 Church

This church desires to fulfill the mandate to reach all people in the context of their immediate community. This is often referred to as the Jerusalem call of Acts 1:8. The church driven by Matthew 28:16-20 often displays a concern to train indigenous leaders and to use them to spread the gospel in a particular context without having to alter church structure or tradition. The issue is primarily one of reaching out to all people and bringing them into the fold of discipleship and development. Theological questions concerning justice and righteousness are not overtly addressed. The primary focus of this church is the missiological imperative to see the lost found and discipled. In spite of this, people do engage in the life of the church and begin to develop relationships that benefit the life and witness of the church in society. The major concerns of this church are individual souls and their eternal well-being. Often this church grows in its multicultural manifestation without compromising the gospel or diluting the truth for the sake of outreach. Ethnicity does not necessarily have a very big influence in the structure of the church. The church continues to maintain tradition and the status quo of years past. Concern revolves around the theme of Matthew 28:19-20 as the Great Commission, and the church probably has a strong evangelical commitment to missions.

Church Model: Bethel Temple Community Bible Church

This congregation meets in the North Philadelphia area often called the "Badlands." Luis Centeno, the pastor, is also a missionary with the American Missionary Fellowship. He comes from the community that he is serving and had worked with youth for over twenty years. Bethel Temple was established in an existing church that was declining in membership due to flight from the community when ethnic transitions occurred.

The ethnic makeup of the congregation is 65 percent Latino (mostly Puerto Rican), 20 percent white and 15 percent black. There are sixty-five members and a general attendance of 190 to 250 people. They have three white and two Latino elders, and there are nine whites and one Latino on the deacon board. Centeno defined the church's understanding of a multiethnic church as follows:

> Because we serve a sovereign Lord and Savior, who has privileged and placed us in this multiethnic community, our goal is to evangelize, congregate and disciple them for the glory and kingdom of God. As a result of this commitment, we have set as one of our biggest goals the destruction of the strongholds of bigotry, prejudice and hatred that show their ugly heads in many multiethnic communities. In these communities there is an uproar as bigotry, prejudice and hatred are prevalent and the people are tired of it. The body of Christ is the only institution that can break the ties that the enemy rejoices in. In being God's channel for healing, we must be careful not to fall into relying on the flesh to do it. Through our Lord and Savior Jesus Christ's power, the church needs to be the very visible and biblical so-

lution. We are commanded to be this in Matthew 28:19-20 and
in Acts 1:8. God shows his compassion to the multitudes in
Matthew 9:35-36, and shows strong integrity in Isaiah 58, and
commands us to do right justice for all people in Micah 6:8.

All of this should be done to give honor and glory to the
Father, Son and Holy Spirit, for all people to praise him.[2]

This ministry is multiethnic throughout, and it finds joy in serving
in diversity. My evaluation of this church shows that over 80 percent of the congregation is poor, having minimal labor skills. The
other 20 percent primarily includes people in full-time ministry
who raise their support in order to function at the church as well
as older whites from outside the community who have white-collar
jobs and enjoy the diversity of Bethel Temple.

The key person in establishing this kind of ministry is the pastor.
The congregation depends on his or her development and experiences. When asked about his commitments to this process of reconciliation, Centeno stated,

What I found definitely was that I had within me a lot of my
old prejudices of these different groups that I was not aware of,
that I was not familiar with. And being with them and getting
to understand that, hey, they are different, they do things different. So, am I willing, as a believer, because of my faith in
Christ, am I willing to die to a lot of my old prejudices so that
Christ can really be seen and present himself through me to the
community as he really is to them—as a people, where he can
identify with them?[3]

Establishing a multiethnic church in the city was not a planned
venture. It just happened to them. The community was looking for
a leader to be for them. This meant, according to my interview, that
they wanted a church to be for all the groups in the community.

The community called for a church to take on the challenge of multiethnicity. Pastor Centeno indicated that moving into a multiethnic church demanded a period of time, a transition. Part of the transition had to do with racial tension that existed in the community. There was violence between the Irish and the Latinos. The city was up in arms trying to control the problem, but to no avail. Centeno indicated that efforts by the city government actually heightened the problem. He said that no one was actually demonstrating the factor of peace and solidarity. An opportunity arose for the church to demonstrate love across cultural lines. This seemed to describe the way in which Centeno ministered. As the opportunity arose, he took on the challenge to show Christ's love across cultural and ethnic lines. This kind of ministry in a community of cultural and racial strife is extremely appealing and has produced enormous numerical growth over the last three years. Centeno stated that people who come to their ministry fall in love with what is going on. "They see the mixture of people, and it's just that oneness of Christ that's going [on]."[4]

Centeno believes that one way to build healthy relationships in a multiethnic situation is to have the congregation eat together. Each person brings a covered dish from his or her culture to share in their meals together. They all get to taste and enjoy part of each culture. Another thing that seems to help the church build relationships is playing and working together. The times to play are extremely enjoyable and provide a unique opportunity for people to see others in a different light. They have learned that recreation is one of the greatest helps to bind people together.

Several aspects of this ministry are striking.

1. Theology lived out. The leaders believe that the sovereign Lord has placed them in this particular community to minister incarnationally. In this case God placed them in a culturally diverse community that needs healing from racial conflict and strife. This is the Lord's calling for the church. The headship of Christ is taken very seriously, as is the biblical position on reconciliation. This church is an evangelical church that depends on Scripture for the direction of the church and its ministry. It also believes strongly in a visible Christian lifestyle. It wants to show evidence of repentance, forgiveness and reconciliation. It also wants to show signs of God's mercy and love.

2. The pastor's preparation. The pastor is equipped with both multicultural experience and an understanding of the precepts of the Word of God in reference to the church and ministry. The pastor who has undergone such experiences and has a deep faith in the Lord can be helpful to the other leaders. I saw in this case that the pastor was the catalyst for the equipping of the other leaders. Discipleship in this situation has taken place primarily through modeling and secondarily through the teaching of Scripture.

3. Trustworthiness. The community depends on the activities of the church, as the church has responded to requests for assistance during hardships. The community has developed a trust in the members of the church and has found this group of believers to be reliable. The church has expanded its ministry to include various outreach programs, such as a substance abuse rehabilitation center, tutoring, an after-school program and a counseling center for family assistance.

4. Evangelistic priority. The church sees its priority as proclaiming the gospel to the unsaved. This mandate takes the church to all the people in the community to share the good news. In this they encounter the rich diversity of the community and see the

Lord's mercy and grace in turning people to himself. This means that people from different ethnic backgrounds will be incorporated into the body. Evangelism in a multiethnic community will result in the growth of diversity in the church.

5. Conflict resolution. Bringing people together from diverse backgrounds inevitably causes conflict. The staff at Bethel Temple is committed to working on personal conflicts. These conflicts are handled through the intervention of a multiethnic staff. Because this community has many broken people, the ministry of counseling and prayer for the congregation becomes a way in which many come to faith in Christ and find Bethel Temple to be a place of refuge. This, as I see it, is an intentional ministry.

6. Flexibility. Due to the diversity that exists in this congregation, the pastor leads with an understanding that there are various ways to worship and to remain faithful to the Scriptures. Centeno provides an environment of freedom and assures the members that they may worship, pray and share in a manner that suits their tradition. This is very helpful in establishing a multiethnic church.

Bethel Temple is a church on the move that ministers in the city incarnationally with a holistic concern for all people and ages.

The Ephesians 2—4 and Luke 4 Church
This church is primarily concerned with correcting the injustices of society and the church by intentionally working toward reconciliation. It embraces other cultures and, in most cases, is a bicultural endeavor in a community where mostly African-Americans live under difficult circumstances. This church displays the realization that the Lord is displeased with ongoing racism in the church and in the U.S. generally.

The Ephesians passages are crucial in that the Lord provides the assurance of his accomplished task of redemption. The Lord has broken down the barriers that separate us. This church is fleshing out the gospel of reconciliation both vertically and horizontally. It wants to see people come to a saving knowledge of the Lord Jesus Christ and grow in relationship to others, breaking down the hostilities that once separated them. Justice and justification are two very important biblical themes in this ministry.

Church Model: Faith Christian Fellowship

Craig Garriott, the pastor of Faith Christian Fellowship, was asked how his church first became multiracial. "It was intentional from the beginning."[5] This ministry is located in Baltimore, a city primarily composed of blacks and whites (approximately 60 percent black and 40 percent white). It is a city that is also divided in its socioeconomic structure. Garriott indicated that "for us the multiracial elements deal with the uniting of different races, particularly with historically alienated groups as well as the socioeconomic classes which are, as a norm, socially alienated in our war of cultures too."[6]

This ministry, which is fourteen years old, has a significant number of biracial and Asian people. In Garriott's view, the worship service is the most crucial hour of the week "just because of the public nature of that hour."[7] The worship service is well represented, with a mixture of leadership leading the service. The pastor's concern is that racial reconciliation will begin to take form through this working together. There is a serious commitment to see the community makeup represented in the church leadership and ministry. There are three styles of worship—gospel from the African-American community, contemporary praise and classical traditional. These styles are repeated throughout the service.

Craig Garriott is no city slicker, but rather a "country boy," as he put it. He came from a homogeneously white, middle-class community and had no crosscultural experiences. He notes, "I was really disillusioned in coming out of a seminary that really was cloning a suburban leadership model and not one dealing with the intensity of issues in the city."[8] It is Garriott's belief that only one who serves out of a deep commitment to Christ and a deep commitment to spiritual development will make it. When asked how he managed to develop the skills to deal with racial friction between African-Americans and whites without any previous crosscultural training, Garriott responded, "Grace—lots and lots of grace. That's the only feature that I know. I've made a lot of mistakes, I still do. Again, [there is] that sense of God's calling and that he will supply. And two men were critical in the early establishment of the church."[9]

Those two men are Bill Bowling and Bob Jenkins. Bill Bowling grew up in the projects of Baltimore City, made it out of a difficult situation and finally went into higher education, where Craig met him and developed a relationship. Craig felt that this kind of person was needed in growing a ministry in this kind of setting. He told us emphatically that without a person like Bowling to help him begin learning community and to assist him in moving ahead, the chances for success would have been slim at best. Bowling had strong African-American roots and was a solid Christian. The other person, Bob Jenkins, was equally important. He was white and was very familiar with the street culture. This brother also had conquered many odds and had provided significant leadership in the church for the last fourteen years.

Garriott stressed that he did not have the ability to accomplish the task alone, but he was helped by the great collaboration of his wife, Maria. The principle communicated was that the leader's spouse should share the leader's long-term commitments, or there could be problems.

Small groups, at the present time, are an important component in this church. Called covenant groups, they spell out all the beliefs and commitments of the small groups and the larger body of Christ. The covenant of reconciliation is adhered to in that the small groups have been established to include an intentional mixture of people. As I reviewed the transcript of the interview with Pastor Garriott, I noticed a constant commitment to building relationship. This begins with the pastor as a model of reconciliation. Asked about his greatest joy, Garriott responded simply, "I think the greatest joy is to feel that you're in the center of God's will. Jesus gives us the prayer to pray—thy kingdom come here on earth as it is in heaven—and when we take a look at heaven, we see how God is uniting all people to himself and to each other, and that really is the picture we're trying to pursue here on earth. I think that we're on moral high ground in one sense in pursuing this. I think it's right."[10]

The Acts 2 Church

This is often the charismatic church that believes God is bringing the multitudes to the cities and that is excited about sharing the gospel through message and signs. Culture is important, but the greater aspect of this ministry is seeing the way the Lord brings diversity together in both forms of ministry and quantity. It is the Pentecost experience over again, and there is immense joy in this manifestation. The intentionality of reconciliation is not as important, owing to the belief that the Holy Spirit will do the work of reconciliation as people worship and serve together. The centrality of this ministry is worship. Worship is where the power is found in this church. This display of adoration toward the Lord attracts many to this church, both Christians and non-Christians. Multicultural dynamics are not intentional. The church, after the fact, usually begins to use the gifts of the different ethnic groups represented.

Church Model: Church In The City

This church displayed a joy in diversity, which it believes the Lord God initiated. In my interview with its plural pastoral staff—one is Jewish, another is African from Nigeria, and the third is a Hispanic native to Denver—the pastors claimed that the Holy Spirit moved this diverse team together. Michael Walker, one of the pastors, stated:

> From the very beginning for us . . . we were involved with a white middle-class church, without judgment on that, and understand that I'm just trying to compare diversity in that. What happened was that we were coming into the city at least three times a week and doing different services out of that church, and what we found was that as we went into these various places, such as shelters, the audience that we were dealing with was very racially mixed. They were either white, Hispanic, American Indian [or] black, and we looked at those sitting out there and realized that there's a common thread that runs through that; it is the need for Christ in their life.[11]

These ministers' concept was to bring the church to the people. They brought worship, teaching, evangelism and healing to the people in the community. As things progressed and they saw the need to establish a ministry with a meeting place in the local setting in order to better firm up the new Christians, a church was established. The people to whom this church was reaching out were the folks that we often consider the "down and out." Many churches do not like reaching out to these poorest of the poor. This church is not intentional about multiethnicity and racial reconciliation. Their primary concern is bringing people to Jesus Christ and allowing the Holy Spirit to incorporate them into the church. Part of their journey to understanding their ministry to the poor and to diverse ethnic groups was promoted by a visit to New York City and David Wilkerson's Times Square Church, which includes fifty-two nationalities. They said that the Lord spoke to them about this kind of ministry, and they knew this is what they were to do.

The Church In The City ministry comes out of the Vineyard movement and has high regard for the use of all the gifts and a great dependence on hearing and responding to the voice of the Lord. It was never their intention to start a church or to see it grow in a multiethnic manner. This they attribute to the work of the Holy Spirit. They often said, "God is sovereign," meaning that God can and should do what he pleases. The three pastors are laymen whom God called to become pastors of this local congregation. Their worship team is diverse, allowing for music and styles of worship that represent the whole congregation. Over and over again there was an expression of amazement on their faces as they talked about what God had done and was doing.

The service is contextualized into both an urban and a culture-specific phenomenon. This ministry, as Walker noted, is "not just having a building that's located in the city, a nice old building or whatever; it's a church with a mission for the city."[12] They depend on modeling. The leaders live in the city and love each other, displaying the kingdom of God in their lifestyles. It is clear that they believe reconciliation will not happen unless God does it, and we must be responsive to his presence. They have a bumper sticker that reads, "Racism is an illness. Only Jesus is the cure." They have intentionally contextualized. They know that if they put a tennis court outside, white kids will come, and if they build a basketball court, African-American kids will join them. They have what they call a hip-hop Friday-night church that reaches the younger generation. When asked why they are pursuing this intentional ministry, they responded that the Lord told them to do it. God continues to speak to his church. If only we would listen!

The Acts 11 and 13 Church

This category deals with churches in transition that are primarily concerned with church renewal and community inclusivism. Acts 11 and 13 indicate a change in the process as some began to speak to Greeks also. It is the church that calls on a team effort to minister to those at Antioch and that establishes a diverse team of leaders (Acts 13:1).

Very often the church in an area of the city that has changed from one culture to another loses members from the existing church over a long period of time and begins to pray for renewal with the coming of a new pastor. The church is desperate but does not want to close its doors. A visionary comes to this ministry with an urban commitment and a willingness to live in the community as a display of the gospel. The church begins to grow with community people, and it also communicates a friendly environment.

Church Model: Dorchester Temple Baptist

This ministry, pastored by the black-white team of Bruce Wall and Craig McMullen, has gone through a cultural and ethnic commu-

nity transition. Once a thriving institution, the church had almost
died. Its long-time pastor left, and, in the words of Pastor
McMullen,

> the church struggled for a period and actually got enough cour-
> age to call their first black pastorate, which was exciting for
> them. . . . This is the step [the previous pastor] would have
> wanted [the church] to take—to turn to a leadership that re-
> flects the community. Unfortunately, many of the Anglo power
> people continued to stay in positions of authority and made it
> very difficult for the fledgling pastor to have a successful time.
> He was there for eighteen months.[13]

Clearly the leaders of this church were deeply concerned about
reflecting the makeup of both the community and the church
without any shortcuts biblically. They came to realize that in order
to have a long-lasting ministry in the community, the church must
have a multiethnic leadership. This church functions with a plu-
rality of leaders who are coequal in authority. The black-white team
reflects the congregation as it is now.

The following statistics provided during our conversation demonstrate the renewal taking place in this church.

> Before we came there were only about fifty folk on a Sunday
> morning with about eighty on the rolls. Of that eighty, about
> 25 percent were Anglo, about 60 percent were black, of which
> 35 percent were kind of Afro-Caribbean and the rest were Afro-
> American, and then the small leftover percentage was Hispanic.
> Since we've come, Sunday-morning service averages between
> 175 and 200 people now, which is an amazing change over one
> year, and the ratio between black and white is almost equal
> now.[14]

The subject of racial reconciliation was brought up. The leadership of this congregation believes that this must be done intentionally, not by chance. McMullen said, "In fact, our church sees itself as an urban church with a neighborhood family focus on a ministry of reconciliation. That's kind of our purpose statement."[15]

Worship styles were somewhat easier to come at because of the diverse leadership and because "there was no real tradition left."[16] The church has been able to represent the various ethnic groups as the church has contextualized its worship services. This is, in the truest sense, a community church—one that takes on the task of reaching all the population groups in the community, from gangs to senior citizens to the many poor surrounding the church.

When asked about the significance of leaders and their training, McMullen immediately highlighted the importance of having leaders who are trained in crosscultural ministries. His own life is marked with numerous crosscultural experiences, and his relationship with his wife has made a strong impact on him. He believes that a pastor who has no crosscultural experiences is a pastor who will probably develop a homogeneous church in a pluralistic community.

A Word of Caution

As we pursue a discussion on the purpose of multiethnic church development, we must be aware of some pitfalls. Some theological and philosophical implications of multiculturalism may lead to the acceptance of various cultures without biblical reflection and dialogue. *Multiculturalism* is a word that is loaded with connotations for the church and society as the church moves ahead without restrictions. Theologians and apologists are concerned with how a concern with multiculturalism can fuel excesses of political correctness.[17] James Davison Hunter speaks of it in his book as *Cul-*

tural Wars: The Struggle to Define America.[18] In his treatise *No Place for Truth,*[19] David Wells argues for a commitment to truth, not culture.

This concern has more to do with the general orientation to multiculturalism than to the particulars. The danger involves our agreeing that only "good" can come out of multiculturalism. Hunter cautions us that "terms seem quite benign, especially to the Christian."[20] He goes on to say, "Aren't we supposed to love our neighbor as ourselves? But then we confront speech codes that criminalize thoughts and words, and we see in others (and perhaps in ourselves) a reluctance to speak out or to take a particular position for fear of being told we are insensitive or perhaps even intolerant."[21]

Multiculturalism can promote a confusing outcome. We are required to love God with all of our being and to love our neighbor as ourselves (Mk 12:30-31), but how that command is incarnated without compromise is sometimes misunderstood. The end or the goal of multiculturalism should not be increased cultural sensitivity or inclusivism so that no one is locked outside the gate (although that is extremely important). Rather, it should be to see the church, by way of multiethnicity, inclusivism and cultural sensitivity, bring about biblical reconciliation, justice and righteousness in the church and in society. Os Guinness in his critique of the church-growth movement and of the more recent megachurch movement indicates, "After all, when the audience and not the message is sovereign, the good news of Jesus Christ is no longer the end, but just the means."[22] That is precisely the point of our concern: will the audience dominate and the authority of the Word become subject to culture?

It is not my intention to develop this thesis of multiculturalism and its implications for modernity or postmodernity and relativism in the context of North America; many who are more able than I have done that task with integrity. It is my concern to recognize its missiological ramifications for justice, church growth and world evangelization.

Conclusion

This chapter has taken the reader through various models that stress or are moved by a particular biblical orientation. The churches are not lopsided, meaning that they do not ignore other responsibilities to which the Scriptures call the church. But, in reference to multiethnicity, the underlying driving force of these ministries may be very specific. The interweaving of all the strands in each model is a learning experience for us as we glean from these pastors their years of experience in crosscultural ministries.

Often I have been asked why I included the short cautionary section on multiculturalism in the last few paragraphs. It seems not to fit, the editors remarked. The caution is part of my conscious effort to allow readers to know that all is not rosy in multiculturalism. Danger lurks about and comes in unexpected clothing, usually growth and success.

Small Group Discussion Questions

1. Very often we allow ourselves to be directed by our comfort zone, which includes our culture and tradition, as to our willingness to meet people who are different from us. Do you need a better handle on what the Scriptures want you to be and to do? If so, what are the biblical considerations in relation to reaching out in love to those who are currently immigrating to this country and may be your neighbors?

2. The models that were provided in this chapter are very interesting, and, for your benefit, you should review them again. Which one of these models do you feel would make a wonderful contribution to your existing ministry? Why have you selected that particular model?

3. On the basis of the models selected for evaluation, what principles came out of this reading that could better equip you to carry out multiethnic ministries? List the principles.

4
MULTI-CONGREGATIONAL CHURCH MODELS

———

*I*MAGINE FOR A MOMENT FOUR OR FIVE DIFFERENT ETHNIC GROUPS with diverse languages entering a sanctuary on a Sunday morning, all between the hours of 9 a.m. and 12 noon. People and more people are entering different sections of the church, trying to direct their families to the right place. Every space in the building is filled, and the commotion is at an all-time high. It sounds complicated, doesn't it? Well, if you were to ask some of the pastors of the church models described in this chapter, I am sure they would say, "You do not know the half of it." At the same time, these leaders would not trade this opportunity of serving the Lord in mutuality for anything in the world. This is the multicongregational church. It seems impossible logistically, but is empowering spiritually.

The multicongregational church and the multiethnic church are the two basic types discussed in this book. Each model that is presented needs to be evaluated on the basis of the information given in chapter three, including consideration of the theological and ecclesiastical traditions of each congregation.

Definition of Multicongregational Church

Peter Wagner defines multicongregational churches as those that minister to several different ethnic groups. If properly managed, they are very effective in urban areas where many different minority groups live in geographical proximity to each other. Some multi-congregational churches simply share facilities with ethnic congregations that maintain their own autonomy, while others go so far as to share the entire church administration equitably.[1]

Jerry Appleby, who has been doing a great deal of research and writing on this subject, defines multicongregational as "any church organization where there is the existence of more than one congregation, whether recognized as separately organized or not. This distinction as a congregation is usually for language reasons but can be for racial or ethnic reasons."[2]

Keith Watkins recently did a study in Los Angeles, and he used the term "multilanguage congregation" to define the multiethnic congregation.[3] The basic purpose in his study was to inform the Christian population of mature models of ministry that are functioning successfully in a complex urban society. Pastor Watkins's concern was to see the church reach out to a community that has drastically changed from "white, native-born, English-speaking" groups to other nationalities and language groups. One of the churches he studied has eight services each Sunday for particular languages and cultures, including an evening service for second-generation Korean youth.

Attempting to define the multicongregational church may be somewhat difficult because of the level of interrelationship expected by each church. Some churches have more interaction among the various language groups than others. What the ethnic groups in a church consider to be sufficient for fellowship and internal growth will depend on the pastors. Also, within each congregation (which is usually considered to be homogeneous) there is a certain amount of diversity. For example, a Hispanic congregation that uses the Spanish language will include people from Central America, South America and the Caribbean. The English-speaking congregation may include many of the second generation from each of the language groups. Several elements were found to be common to many of the multicongregational churches.

1. The multicongregational church uses one facility for several language groups (congregations).

2. Language, more than anything else, seems to be what keeps congregations separated. There are certainly cultural issues, but language is what most churches indicated as the dividing line.

3. There are different levels of interinvolvement in each congregation. Some churches come together more often than others.

4. Usually the English-speaking church owns the church building and determines the use of the facilities and the events for any kind of combined effort. The other language groups tend to go along with the requests from the English-speaking church.

5. There is very little sharing of ministry projects. This is not always true, but it seems to be more common than not.

Two of the churches I visited during my research, First Baptist Church of Flushing, New York, and First Church of the Nazarene of Los Angeles, are, in my opinion, models that provide the best demonstration of how to support both biblical commitments and sociological issues. Both of the churches provide alternatives in terms of ownership and of sharing ministry projects.

The following definition is a working definition for those of us who are interested in developing such models: *The multicongregational church is a church that has taken on the challenge of biblical justice and missions in the context of racial strife and increased pluralism. It builds relationships between the different language groups, intent on bringing biblical reconciliation between them. This display of the kingdom of God motivates multi-language congregations to come together and to restructure the present monocultural formation of the church into one that is based on obedience to the Word of God. The multicongregational church provides for both autonomy and interdependency.*

There are three key models of multicongregational churches: (1) renting model, (2) celebration model and (3) integrative model.

The Renting Model

Many of us are familiar with this model. It is common in our urban context where many immigrants are trying to settle down and start a new life with their families. This model provides ethnic groups with facilities on a rental basis, primarily for use on a Sunday morning and evening. The "landlord" church rents the facilities as a ministry to its community, which has undergone ethnic transition. It is the church's way of doing ministry to new people groups that have immigrated to this country and have, for the time being, moved into its urban area. The church very often speaks of this involvement as a worthy ministry of compassion that serves minorities that have specific needs in getting started in their new ministry.

At times the renting model is also considered a means to church growth and crosscultural ministry. In many cases the existing church is losing numbers due to death and migration out of a culturally transitional community; a sense of hopelessness pervades the church. Other groups' use of the facilities provides a spark that has been missing for years. It also provides the church with additional income.

Relationships are usually superficial and begin with polite and caring discussions that express the pastor's concern to "help" others. Within a short period of time, six months or less, the conflicts begin to appear. A problem typically begins with disagreement on building maintenance. One group, the owner of the building, has a long history in the facility and has memories of many wonderful experiences of the past. The sanctuary, in particular, is to be respected and cared for by all who use the building. The group that is renting may view use of the facility differently, and this brings a certain amount of strain to the relationship. The "honeymoon" is over. The newcomers are now seen as trespassers who are insensitive to the values of the existing church. The irritation is compounded when the owner tells the groups that are leasing how they should manage their children.

This model is presented by denominations as a multiethnic congregation, but in reality the relationships are not stable and never go beyond the renting stage to achieve mutual accountability. Therefore, this cannot be considered a multiethnic congregation.

This model presents few opportunities to work on relationships or to resolve issues. The primary reason is that the owning congregation has only one goal in mind, and that is to utilize the property in a manner that will help other groups until they find their own building or decide to become part of the existing congregation through denominational affiliation. The owner tells the leasing group what is expected of it as long as it continues to rent the facilities. There are some opportunities for combined efforts and celebration, but this is not considered a long-range goal. The church does seem busy and active, and this provides the owner church with a certain sense of hope and potential growth. Denominations very often boast that "there are four language groups" meeting in a particular church. This boasting may include a numerical disclosure that seems to imply that the church is growing, when in fact there is no growth at all. The group that is leasing is merely in transition, hoping to find its own facility.

Very often there is mutual exploitation, the owner church prospering through superficial growth and the renting church hoping that the owner church will eventually turn over the facility to it. Before we disown this model, we must regard it as a possible model of ministry for a church located in a multiethnic community. Several elements are necessary to achieve a process that provides for healthy, long-term relationships.

1. Clearly define the relationship at the outset. We need to be more intentional concerning our goals for multiethnic ministries. What are the Christian reasons for the relationship as well as the missiological reasons? The expectations of both congregations should be laid out and evaluated periodically to see if there is a need to adjust the initial commitment. It is most important that Christian attitudes be exercised. Too often the relationship is reduced to that of a worldly landlord and tenant.

2. The pastors should lead the way by displaying concern for one another. Pastors getting together to pray for the needs of their congregations and families is a helpful exhibition of how the church should act toward one another. This presentation of love

should continue, beginning with the leaders and moving throughout the congregations.

3. Learning together is also helpful. The Lord has brought these two or more congregations together, and they need to follow the Lord's direction and begin to share the values and histories of each culture. Services may be combined in order to allow the different congregations to have liberty in bringing their uniqueness to worship and to the teaching of the Word. This sharing will build a deeper understanding of God's body throughout the world.

4. As expectations change and move toward some kind of affiliation, the leadership should proceed to describe the new direction the churches have taken. The churches may remain independent, but they can relate closely in outreach and in providing assistance to each other. Others may decide to join the denomination associated with the owning church.

The Celebration Model

This model invites other ethnic groups that may or may not be leasing the church facilities to participate in the life of the church. It desires more than a leasing relationship. The inviting church would like to have more of a relationship with other groups and would like to see growth in its congregation through encouraging the second generation of the other congregations to attend its services. This model has several combined services for the purpose of demonstrating the kingdom of God active in a world filled with racial strife. One leader in my research stated:

We have a Laotian group; we have a Cambodian group; we have a Spanish group; and these people meet during Sunday with their groups—they have their own Sunday-school classes; they have their own services—but once a month we get together, like our Communion Sunday. And for some reason, you see the congregation—it is . . . made up of different colors, different shapes, different sizes, and I like to believe that is what heaven is going to look like.[4]

That church will have several occasions to get together, such as Christmas, Easter and the anniversaries of the church. The one component in the celebration model that leaves something to be desired is that the inviting church usually has no intention of sharing the ownership of the church. The decision-making body guards control over what happens in the church. One individual indicated during my research that "our white folk will be in power for a long time. They have an awfully hard time seeing the value of the ethnicity and the contribution that ethnicity could make."[5]

Several characteristics of the celebration model were identified.

1. It has a long history, is very proud of its past accomplishments and tries to continue that heritage. It may have been a pulpit-centered church that was blessed with some of the best preachers and expositors. This is what the church became known for, and it will not want to make any changes that would detract from that reputation. A church may have a strong worship core with music that is culturally unique. Again, the church will want to stay with that tradition and will resist change for whatever reason.

2. This church also has a mission core to its philosophy of ministry and wants to reach out to others without losing its own uniqueness. Evangelism is important, and "winning souls" is a high priority.

3. There is a paternalistic dimension, since the owning church maintains its culture and tradition.

4. Control is very evident in this church, even if the people now attending the church are not part of the tradition, are from a

different culture, and outnumber those in the existing church. Even if, for example, the church is only 20 percent Anglo, that element may retain the power.

This model has the potential to become useful in a multiethnic context. It may profit from the diversity in the congregation as it leads to numerical growth. But the church should take the following steps into consideration.

1. Create a mission statement that is grounded on Scripture and is committed to contextualization in a multiethnic community.

2. Address with church leadership the issue of biblically restructuring the church's philosophy of ministry. Do this after completing research work, such as demographics.

3. As the church engages other ethnic groups to establish a relationship, use the mission and doctrinal statements of the church as tools for discussion and reformation. The churches will begin to discover their similarities and dissimilarities through the study of these documents. Some churches have discovered, after numerous years of working together, that their positions on the subject of multiethnicity are quite different. It would have been helpful for them to know this at the outset of their relationship.

4. The churches must have honest discussions on ownership, control and future aspirations. This will provide for the inclusion and affirmation of each group's vision for the future. Every one of the members is important to the direction of the church and should have ample opportunity to express his or her vision. This should also include such subjects as theological commitments. It is unsafe to make assumptions about what people believe and how they see the multiethnic church theologically.

The Integrative Model

The integrative model is not solely concerned with seeing people of various ethnic groups come together. It also wants to see them influence the life and structure of the church. I have chosen two churches as integrative models, one in New York and the other in Los Angeles, two of the seven major receiving cities for immigrants. Both churches have a number of congregations that use different languages in their services, but they all belong to the same denomination. This denominational affiliation, in my opinion, makes the process much smoother, and goals for racial and ethnic reconciliation become much more attainable.

Church Model: First Church of the Nazarene

First Church of the Nazarene of Los Angeles was founded in 1890 by Phineas F. Bresee in downtown Los Angeles. This mission movement established the Church of the Nazarene denomination. In 1960 the Sunday attendance at First Church of the Nazarene was

> in the 600 range, and represented people in the upper middle class. . . . When the demographic changes began, this congregation faced the transition sooner and faster than was the case in most other congregations in the area. In 1973 Ron Benefiel came to the church's staff to work with young adults. He continued in that post for six years and then was off staff for two. In 1982 he returned as pastor and has continued in that position since then.[6]

This brief history helps to explain the base from which the church moved into a concern for an integrative model of ministry that embraced justice as one of its major goals for the life of the church in a diversified and racially torn community. Ron Benefiel, a sociologist with a Ph.D. from the University of Southern California, began to see the partnering of theology and sociology as being extremely important. "Sociology by itself can describe what is happening but cannot provide direction for change. Theology can provide purpose but by itself does not connect very well with the real world in which the church is living. Together they make a strong partnership."[7]

This dialogue between sociology and theology in an inner-city community reestablished the church's commitment to the poor. First Church of the Nazarene includes four congregations—English, Spanish, Filipino and Korean. Each congregation meets with its own language group but also has many opportunities to meet with the others as a combined staff and congregation. Watkins noted, and my interview with Pastor Benefiel affirmed, that there is independence among the groups and yet a wonderful display of biblical unity. The interdependence was mutual; each congregation needed the others and relied on the gifts and resources of each church. "Benefiel talks of one church and four congregations."[8]

As already pointed out, the denominational relationship makes this process much more workable. All of the language groups are recognized by the Church of the Nazarene denomination as autonomous congregations. The numbers in each congregation have changed, but no recent recording was available. The English congregation has about 250 people, the Spanish has slightly more than 250, the Filipino has 60, and the Korean has about 100 people attending on Sunday morning. The eldership from each of the congregations controls this church. It is called the Multicongregational Council and has fourteen members, including representatives from each congregation. "The number of representatives for each congregation is determined annually by a formula that includes each congregation's income, average attendance, and total membership."[9]

All of the congregations have a focus of ministry to serve the parish in which the church finds itself. However, it is not exclusive to the community; all of the groups maintain ministries and Bible studies in other communities as a means of outreach. They are all committed to church growth through evangelism. The four congregations have mutual ministries, such as a Christian day school and a parish nursing component. There are also distributions of food and other ministries of mercy that are done with personnel from each of the congregations. The budget for the church, including the school and ministries of the nonprofit Bresee Foundation, that was disclosed to Watkins in his research was $1.7 million.[10]

The most unusual aspect of this ministry is the willingness of the congregations not only to share the facilities but also to own the building mutually. The four congregations have equal ownership of the church facilities, which includes full sharing of all the responsibilities and overhead. The congregations and pastors went through a process of meeting together for a period of time to review the meaning of sharing and owning the property. The final part of this process was a celebration service, which included signing a declaration that the four congregations now legally owned the church building that was once owned solely by the English-speaking congregation of the First Church of the Nazarene. This change of ownership celebration occurred while I was in California doing my research. The congregations had a worship service in which they all shared in preaching the Word and leading the worship. The different languages were used with translation. All of this culminated in signing the legal papers, sharing the Lord's Supper, and fellowshiping over a multiethnic meal outside in the community.

This was an exciting and wonderful time for all the congregations and for those of us who saw history in the making.

In my interview with Benefiel I was interested in discussing the components of his philosophy of ministry. His response to me was similar to the following five principles, which were given to Watkins.

Community in mission is the first principle. Both elements have to be present, for community without mission is unfaithful to the gospel, but mission without community leads to burnout. A second principle is ministry to the parish, which is understood to be a specific geo-political unit. In the case of First Church of the Nazarene, this territory extends in a two-mile radius [around] the church. The third principle is that ministries are to be holistic. They start at some point of need, such as hunger, but seek to build bridges from these points of need to other aspects of one's life, including the relationship with God. A fourth principle is that ministry is contextual and incarnational. The church no longer is a[n outside] missionary [enterprise] to the city but it embraces the city, is part of the city. It must always start where people are in their life settings. The fifth principle is that the church is to be a kingdom resource. Not only does it have building and staff to offer the community, but this church can be a teaching church to help many other people also learn to be in mission in the city.[11]

The principles presented by Pastor Benefiel were affirmed by the other leaders of the congregations. They were most enthusiastic over a model of ministry that helped their denomination move out of its cultural walls and suburban mindset. They realized that churches have options when cultural and ethnic transitions take place. A congregation can keep other people out of its church, it can relocate and move into a more homogeneous community, or it can reach out to the new people groups in the community.

One point made by one of the pastors was that the transition for second generation is easier in a multicongregational setting where they all meet in the same facility. Young people who are becoming more comfortable with the English language can attend the English-speaking church. This can be an advantage when the young people enjoy a multiethnic worship setting; it may not be an advantage if it separates families and denies the first-generation congregation the benefits of having new experiences presented to them.

As I evaluated this church, I noticed several distinguishing points.

1. Plural pastors can minister to each other and can enrich one another in the study of the Word and in their views of adoration and worship.

2. As congregations minister crossculturally, their members find growth in their personal lives and experience sanctification in a manner too often ignored. Some find that their perception of others is paternalistic and racist. As the congregations engage in ministry, Christians repent of their ungodly views and feel a fresh desire to learn from each other, declaring their need for their brothers and sisters.

3. The church is growing both quantitatively and qualitatively. It has been the argument of some from the Fuller School of Church Growth that churches do not grow in a multiethnic setting. My discovery is that the churches I evaluated are all growing, and it seems to me that they would have died in their present context if not for their willingness to embrace the call of the sovereign God to reach out to new people groups in their communities.

4. The headship of Christ is more visible. Dependency on Christ as head of the church is vivid and appealing to the people of God in that church. I sensed in them a great awareness of the teaching of Scripture in matters of faith and of obedience to the relationship between Christ and the church.

5. The Great Commission as taught in the Gospel of Matthew is part of the church, not just part of a mission committee of the church that delegates the responsibility to a mission society or its denomination in forms of money distribution. In this case God's people are engaged in missions.

6. The community has a kingdom testimony of people from diverse backgrounds being loved and being accepted and then sharing their possessions for the purpose of advancing God's kingdom. This testimony is uncommon in a society where racial strife is more evident than brotherly love. While it often leads to evangelism and growth in the church, it also provides for healing in the community.

7. The biblical notion of unity in diversity is fleshed out in this biblical order of the church.

There are several reasons why I believe this church has developed into one that exemplifies the integrative model of multicongregational churches. The Anglo pastor, often considered the senior pastor, is committed to a biblical understanding of the kingdom of God. He is aware that Scripture is sufficient for the task and is desirous of being obedient to the lordship of Christ. Scripture is the authority for the life of the church. The pastors of the other congregations are open to the call for biblical reconciliation and justice and are willing to spend time working through the implications of how reconciliation can take place in their setting. The congregations are mission-oriented. They seek to see the community come to a saving knowledge of Christ. This allows them to do outreach among the many different ethnic groups in their parish.

The community is diverse and keeps the congregations aware of its needs. The church maintains a Christian day school, which affords it an opportunity to meet many of the parents of the community. The church provides various ministries that assist many of the people coming into the community. The church has many links into the community that help the church to grow and to grow in cultural diversity.

Church Model: First Baptist Church

McKenzie Pier, who did a research paper on First Baptist Church of Flushing, New York, named this church "Heaven's Mirror in Flushing, New York."[12] My own contact with the staff of First Baptist Church led me to concur with Pier that this is a wonderful display of God's love and light in a world of much confusion and struggle.

Flushing, New York, is a very diverse community. There are over 104 language groups, with a population in 1990 of 250,000 people. This borough of New York has undergone what Ray Bakke calls the Asianization phenomenon. In the seven years from 1980 to 1987 the Asian community grew from 10 percent to 50 percent of the total population. During this same period the Anglo community dropped from 80 percent to 35 percent. The Hispanic and black communities stayed the same.[13] The First Baptist Church of Flushing took on the challenge of not only a transitional community but also a multilanguage community.

This Conservative Baptist church has a long history of effective ministry in the Flushing Queens area, having been established in 1856. In 1978 a new senior pastor was called to a congregation of

142 members. Soon after, a Chinese congregation came into being with approximately 120 members. Interestingly enough, this Chinese church had no denominational ties with the Conservative Baptists. By 1990 the church consisted of four language groups—English, Spanish, Chinese and Portuguese—that are considered interdependent congregations with their own pastors.[14] More recently the Portuguese congregation combined with the Spanish congregation, and a Filipino fellowship has begun. Another important development is that the church considers itself one church with different language groups. The staff works together as a team rather than as independent groups making their own decisions. The purpose statement of the church reads, "The purpose of First Baptist Church of Flushing is to worship God through a loving unified body of multi-ethnic believers trained to witness the Word of God to the World of God."[15]

In my interview I asked Pastor Rosser why the church is a multiethnic church. He identified a theological reason: Christ came to bring reconciliation with God as well as with one another.

> The model of the New Testament reflects an urban, multiethnic church from Pentecost right through to differences in Greek/Hebrew communities in Jerusalem. [It] demonstrates eventual oneness (empowerment to select leaders). [In the] Antioch church walls are broken down and Paul and Barnabas bring together people of Syria, North Africa, etc. There is where they were first called Christians, so the sign of Christianity is heterogeneity.[16]

As Pastor Rosser also stated, "It was in the 1960s when the pastors determined that the church was going to move from missions to mission—foreign to present community concerns. At this point the church split; 75 percent of the people left, and those who stayed opened up the church. Four years later the Chinese came in and eventually the Hispanic congregation."[17] The design and intent was not to rent to other groups but rather to build a body that is confessional, Christocentric, focused on the core and not the boundaries, and to really become intentional in heterogeneity.[18]

The Hispanic pastor indicated that one of the most helpful elements in this process was respect for each other. "Not everything is a rose, but we never walk away without coming back to the table for reconciliation. . . . We respect Christians in the body more than where they come from."[19] The Chinese pastor stated that most come to the church because they agree with the church's philosophy.[20] It was clear in our group discussion that all of the pastors agreed that there is really no homogeneous group. Even the English-speaking church has people from forty countries, representing four continents. Most speak English as a second language. Those who are second or third generation use English as a primary language.

I was intrigued by the love that the church leaders had for each other and by their enormous mutual respect. I asked how the groups came together. One leader mentioned that space was an issue, and it was becoming more and more difficult to meet together as one group. Even so, they try to have common services on special holidays such as Thanksgiving, Christmas and Easter. They also meet for special events such as baptisms and mission conferences. An exciting project that promoted a display of unity was the production of a play, *The Choice*. The different language groups took part in developing the play. A strong bond was built out of the need for rehearsals and prayer. It seemed to most of the leaders that very often working together, rather than worshiping together, leads to growth in awareness of each other and to the most learning about each other. Church members also do a great deal of evangelism in the community. This makes an unusual impression in a community that is very divided along cultural and linguistic lines.

When I visited the church, the Chinese pastor had just returned from the Ukraine. The staff believes that it is important for each leader and congregation member to have outside exposure to other ethnic groups. This is accomplished through travel in connection with missions to a foreign country. A mission team is made up of Christians from each of the language groups. This heterogeneous group ministers alongside a church in another country. This experience facilitates significant growth and bonding among the various groups.

What has made this group a healthy and growing multicongregational church is that the different congregations hold to a common theological position and mission commitment. The staff, which is made up of the pastors from each language congregation and other leaders from each group, is committed to biblical unity and intentional biblical mission.

As the church leaders work together on growing the church, there must be numerous times when frictions and tensions dominate the meeting. I asked how they dealt with conflict. The staff responded by noting that it takes time, first of all, to learn how to work together. "We allow each other to say whatever they want to say. There is freedom to speak. . . . The original intent is very clear—we are not coming here to share a facility, but we are ministering as a team. . . . [We] learn to hear each other's heart, not just words. Relationship takes a lot of time and art."[21]

One of the staff members from the Hispanic congregation remarked interestingly that the mission of the church is understood right down to the members of the congregation. Their goal is to live out the Great Commission. "Our goal is heaven for all in the community."[22] Rosser noted several points that are significant to the life of the church. The first is transformation, lives being redeemed and changed. The second is mobilization of those people, having them exercise spiritual gifts to be used for one another. The third is a sense of community fellowship, people enjoying each other. He then wanted to go beyond that by including (1) revival, the renewal of the church here and in the cities in the Northeast, (2) reconciliation within the local church but also reconciliation in the community, in the nation and in the world, and (3) church reconstruction, enabling other churches to catch that vision and preparing leadership with that kind of vision, especially in the seminary with which the Flushing church is involved.

The staff felt it would be very difficult to effect that kind of transformation; the best that most churches can do is collect money for foreign missions. It is too difficult for churches to break through ethnocentrism. The Asian group indicated that it was a problem for some of the Asian churches to break through their ethnocentrism; they have no desire to minister crossculturally. Others felt that missionaries carry the wrong agenda into the mission field and that the root of the problem is the church and its teaching and life.

The Flushing church carries out its commitment to discipline in the church. Rosser noted, "There is church discipline that is in place to see that life matches our doctrine. We have exercised church discipline in all three congregations. It's a little harder (and more drawn out) in the Chinese congregation because of the issue of 'losing face,' but it's still done."[23] The point here is that while church discipline remains a high priority for all the groups, the way of handling that discipline must be contextualized. There must be a special sensitivity in the Chinese congregation, which, while sharing the same quality of discipline exercised in the other congregations, still allows the individual to "save face."

A definition of the multiethnic church was shared by the pastors, in particular Pastor Rosser: "A group of twice-born people committed to biblical understanding who are very missional, committed to the Great Commission of ministering together unto the Lord and to one another and to their community with the goal of expanding the Kingdom of God."[24]

During the time I spent at Flushing First Baptist Church, I discovered the following dimensions in the church that are helpful in understanding the integrative model.

1. Its staff of Christians was committed to the gospel in word and life, understanding the need for reconciliation between people and God as well as between people and people. They felt that it was inconsistent to be Christian and not to love your neighbor, no matter what his or her background. The pastoral staff was made up of men who modeled redemptive lives for their congregations as they worked at reconciliation, evangelism and edification.

2. There is no one individual who makes this process of reconciliation happen in a manner that glorifies the Lord. As I see it, the success of this church is due to the pastoral staff's willingness to obey Scripture at all cost. The pastors have been together since the late 1970s, sufficient time to wrestle through the issues while continuing to see the biblical ideal as relevant for today. The great stress on pluralism leads them to utilize the Scriptures more in seeking to understand how the Lord is working and how the church is to carry out its mandate.

3. It is clear to me that the context in which the church finds

itself and the commitment the church makes in reference to its mission is important. In this case the church made an important decision to serve the community in which it houses its congregations. The community became the context for mission, and this was a matter of obedience to the will of the sovereign Lord.

4. Pastors always, in my opinion, play the key role in determining whether or not the ministry in its context is successful. In this case the pastors and staff are Christians who love people and the Word of God. It is inspiring to see how much they love each other.

5. The mission commitments, particularly the call to the Great Commission, were taken seriously by the church leaders. These commitments were part of the everyday life of the church, not just slogans for the yearly missionary conferences.

6. Church growth was evident. The staff spoke highly of conversion growth, which meant that they preached and baptized new believers, incorporating them into the church. The church was growing beyond its capacity to house all the new members. Church growth does happen in a heterogeneous context, but church growth for the sake of church growth was not part of their agenda. The glory of God was held preeminent in all that they did.

7. Justice was a biblical teaching that was to be adhered to by all Christians, and this meant that racism, oppression and the needs of the poor were dealt with in order to satisfy the Lord of the harvest. This also meant that holistic ministries and services of mercy were carried on by each of the language groups.

Conclusion
It is important to note that the integrative model that is presented in this chapter does not end with integration or any description of assimilation. Rather, it moves toward fleshing out Scripture in

matters of reconciliation and justice, a maturity in the body of Christ that captures the essence of Paul's message in Ephesians 2:11-22 and 4:14-16. Models of ministry are tested not on the basis of context alone but rather on biblical precepts. The two together assist us not only in establishing ministries in diverse communities but also in continuous evaluation of them. This tension is never eased and probably should be accepted as ongoing.

Small Group Discussion Questions

1. The definitions provided in this chapter are not engraved in stone. How do you feel about the definitions given? Explain your reasons for accepting or changing some of the definitions.

2. There are three multicongregational models in this chapter that seem to be logical and easy to understand. Which of the three do you think your church could work with? Why?

3. Have any of you been in a ministry that demonstrated some of the characteristics exhibited in the models in this chapter?

4. What are other possibilities for doing multiethnic ministries?

5

MULTIETHNIC CHURCH MODELS

---

*M*OST VIDEOS THAT SPEAK TO THE ISSUE OF RACIAL RECONCILIA-
tion (e.g., *Face to Face* from InterVarsity Press) promote the
church that has begun to win the battle of isolation (e.g., Rock
of Our Salvation Church, Chicago). Racism and bigotry are overcome in the multiethnic church. This is the picture of a white hand
clasping an African-American hand, both lifted high to God in
praise. It is what we all want, isn't it? At least this is what the video
is selling. It seems to us, as Christians, that this is what God
wants—to see diverse people in one place at one time worshiping
God together. This group of worshiping people is what we term the
"multiethnic church."

The multiethnic church includes culturally diverse people who
meet together as one congregation, utilizing one language, usually
English. This kind of congregation, which meets on Sunday morn-

ings with numerous ethnic and racial groups on display, is often taken for granted. "How wonderful it is to see so many different cultures worshiping together!" we exclaim. But we hardly ever wonder how this feat is accomplished or whether the crosscultural dynamic is difficult to maintain. Although the multiethnic church is the church that we are often familiar with and find to be the most exciting, it is also the most difficult in reference to embracing and maintaining people from diverse cultural backgrounds.

Definition of Multiethnic Church

Definitions of the MEC were easy to come by. But as I studied the definitions submitted by the people from whom I solicited them, I discovered that there were numerous dissimilarities. Five definitions, which are included in the appendix, were particularly helpful. All of them identified the necessity of having a "significant presence" from at least two distinct ethnic groups. One definition specifically excluded a congregation that is primarily composed of a single ethnic group but includes a few assorted others. There was some disagreement about how this might look. One person saw a multiethnic church bringing together members of two distinct ethnic backgrounds to interact as one congregation that utilizes a common third culture. Another respondent rejected the notion of what he termed an "osterized" mixture. He was more interested in seeing all the diversity displayed. A third person specified that the physical environment (i.e., room decor) should fully reflect the diversity. Some respondents brought up structural issues. One wanted to see all groups fully participating as members *and* ministers. Another wanted to be sure that no single tradition dominated in any area. One respondent specifically dealt with structural changes necessary to assure the continuation of diversity. To him this meant the church had to be intentional in its approach to multiethnicity.

I received many other definitions, but only one specifically identified reconciliation as part of the multiethnic church process. This does not mean that the others excluded reconciliation from their understanding of the development of the MEC. Rather, it suggests either that they assume reconciliation to be an integral part of the MEC or that they have not had sufficient opportunity to review the subject. Glen Kehrein of Circle Urban Ministries in Chicago stated in an interview that reconciliation was the very reason for having an MEC.[1] In this case the intentionality of justice was overt, and it was the driving force for their ministry.

Qualitative and Quantitative Dimensions

Taken together, the definitions provided both quantitative and qualitative dimensions. The quantitative dimension primarily deals with the numerical makeup of the ethnic groups that meet together. The numerical percentages of each group represented determines whether or not a particular church is an MEC. There must be sufficient representation of any particular ethnic group in order to claim that a church is multiethnic. It is not enough to have a smattering of one culture or another. Some of the respondents indicated that a certain percentage of any one group was necessary.

To understand the quantitative aspect of the MEC, we can look at the Tremont Temple Baptist Church in Boston, which describes its church as 33 percent African-American, 2 percent Laotian, 10 percent Latino, 5 percent Cambodian, and 50 percent Anglo. The makeup of the Rock of Our Salvation Church in Chicago is 70 percent African-American and 30 percent Anglo. Both churches meet the quantitative requirements for being an MEC.

The numerical makeup of an MEC is a determining factor, but it is not the only one. Both churches just mentioned have more to their ministries than percentages. They also hold significant commitments to the qualitative dimension, which is the aspect of the church that refers to the life and organization of the local ministry. In terms of the qualitative dimension, the church has biblically contextualized its ministry to the multiethnic context in which it finds itself demographically. This includes reforming the structure or administration of the body to represent the church biblically in the same way it did when it was a homogeneous church.

Thus the effective MEC is more than just a variety of cultures meeting together under one roof. The qualitative dimension is essential, having to do with the life of the church as well as the organization of the ministry. How are each of the ethnic groups represented and involved in the formation of the life of the church? Does the organization (or, as Lupton terms it, the "structure") of the church involve or allow for the actual membership of the church to lead and to direct the ministry God has given to the congregation? It may be that structural change will have to represent the cultural mix of that congregation, but this cannot be done without a clear understanding that the Bible provides the necessary tension for that formulation.

The qualitative aspect also has to do with matters of reconciliation and justice. It is important that the church understand the goal of the MEC. Maintaining ethnic diversity in a local church is part of the MEC, but it is not an end in itself. Remember our earlier caution in regard to multiculturalism. S. D. Gaede notes,

Multiculturalism also carries much baggage that ought to worry Christians. This baggage has less to do with the details of mul-

ticulturalism than with its general orientation. And perhaps the
best way to get at this is to notice that more and more, those
who favor multiculturalism argue not on the basis of a desire for
justice but on the basis of multiculturalism's practical necessity
or its validity as a general worldview.[2]

If the goal is to have ethnic presence and no more, we primarily
have a quantitative model, and this will be measured by how many
different ethnic groups are represented. Forty different ethnic
groups may be attending the church but not participating in the
formation and distribution of the power and authority of the
church. The structure could very well be the same as it has been
for the last fifty years, even though the context of its mission has
changed. This was true of one church I visited in New York City.
The congregation was made up of many ethnic groups, but the
structure of the church and the pastoral staff had not changed
since the church's founding. Justice and racial reconciliation did
not concern the church's leadership. The qualitative aspect was
missing. Members of different ethnic groups voiced their concern
about this lack of consideration from the pastoral staff. Attention
needed to be given to the installation of multiethnic leaders and
to the contextualization of their perspective on worship and on the
ministry of the Word.

Gaede directs our attention to Jesus. "The problem with the
pragmatic approach to multicultural sensitivity, then, is that it
rules out Jesus' approach. It says that the end is cooperation, good
relations, harmony and agreement. And it thereby undermines and
displaces the true ends of human existence."[3] It is my opinion that
both quantitative and qualitative dimensions are necessary for an
MEC to be effective in reaching out to a community that is ethnically diverse and growing in this diversity. Presence of the multi-

ethnic community in the local church is a given if mission is applied, but presence without incorporation limits the process of true biblical discipleship. The qualitative dimension occurs as participants are discipled and become responsible members of the local ministry. It is a state of incompleteness when the church neglects to train and incorporate believers into the fullness of the ministry. "The Hispanic educator Arturo Madrid states, 'Diversity is desirable only in principle, not in practice. Long live diversity—as long as it conforms to *my* standards, to *my* mind set, to *my* view of life, to *my* sense of order.' "[4]

Two churches exemplify both the quantitative and qualitative aspects of MEC development.

Church Model: International Bible Church

The International Bible Church, an independent evangelical church located in Los Angeles, is composed of "Anglos, American Indians, Asian Indians, Blacks, Chinese, Guatemalans, Filipinos, Koreans, Mexicans, Salvadorans, Russians, Taiwanese, Thais and Ukraine."[5] The pastor, Mark Oh, is a Korean who is committed to world evangelism. Oh had originally planned to return to Korea to do church planting after completing his studies at Fuller Theological Seminary, but he remained in California to pastor this church.

Pastor Oh holds firmly to the belief that the "churches in Rome and Galatia were racially mixed and cross-cultural."[6] He also believes that Jesus' ministry was crosscultural from the beginning.[7] Oh finds scriptural support for pursuing multiculturalism and crosscultural ministry in the church today.

The International Bible Church was founded in March 1972 with thirty-two members "on the conviction that when the risen Lord commanded His disciples to make disciples of all nations *(panta ta ethne),* He meant all ethnic groups (without regard of color, race, language, and national origin) of the world."[8] It was the understanding of this group that if people of different origins came to live in the community of the church, the local ministry must reach out and allow what Oh calls "Christ culture" to transcend ethnic differences so that they could minister together, live in harmony and learn from each other as children of God. This rationale has been the foundation of the International Bible Church.

Oh indicates that the one purpose of the church is to glorify God (Eph 1:5-6, 12, 14). He notes that this is done through the ministry of making disciples of all nations and equipping them to do the work of the ministry, building up the saints of the local church (Eph 4:11-16). This is accomplished through what he calls the "agent of the Word of God." Therefore, the fundamental task of the church becomes teaching the Word of God. Another assumption of this church is found in Galatians 3:28: "There is neither Jew nor Greek, slave nor free, male nor female, for you are all one in Christ Jesus." Oh's understanding of this passage is that "in Christ, who is the paradigm of lived transcendence, . . . the believers can . . . follow in His steps, transcending all human distinctions to reach others for Jesus Christ."[9] Those who are in Christ can set aside their differences and barriers and serve and worship together because they are the "new humanity."

When International Bible Church began its ministry, it opened its doors to all groups. The original members were not satisfied with the existing monocultural profile of the church in their context. They saw it as a matter of spiritual maturity to be able to look beyond their culture and open their lives to new experiences. As they visited the community, it became clear that the people in the parish were of diverse ethnic backgrounds. The church invited all to come and worship. Many came to the services and brought their uniqueness to bear on the formation of the church. The language used was English. "Unlike some of the bilingual churches which have to translate their services, one of the benefits of the multiethnic church like ours is the use of one common working language—English."[10] The members understood that this would neglect recent immigrants who might be unable to understand English.

There are many interracial marriages in this church, including Oh's marriage. Here again is the uniqueness of the context. Los Angeles lends to interracial marriages, and the church that welcomes this kind of diversity will become home for many in the area. At the same time, the pastor realizes that this kind of church will not be for everyone.

An interesting aspect of this church is that it is committed to multiethnicity as a fulfillment of Scripture. The Word of God determined its position in regard to the multiethnic church. It also believes that the church is born providentially in the tension of a multiethnic community. Oh asks, "How then is a multiethnic church born? It is born in a time of need, situation, and environment in a multiethnic neighborhood. . . . We who live and minister in the inner city neighborhoods cannot avoid multiethnicity today. That is the real America of Los Angeles."[11]

In my interview with him, Oh indicated that he saw only this kind of church as being multiethnic in the truest sense. The multicongregational church described earlier in this book, in his opinion, is not a multiethnic church, since it would not have to deal with the tension of ongoing interfacing and working together. My research did not demonstrate this. The different language groups of the multicongregational churches worked together on various levels. The English-speaking congregations of many multicongregational churches are MECs in their own right. The spirit of inclusivity that contributes to the healthy development of an MEC is the same spirit that contributes to a healthy multicongregational church.

The International Bible Church has two ministry priorities.

[The first priority is] to preach the gospel of Jesus Christ to all ethnics with whom we come in contact, so that these ethnics may become discipled Christians. Evangelism is the top agenda of our ministry. This priority is carried out by personal contacts, public worship services, home Bible study groups, and home mission outreach in the neighborhood and foreign mission outreach through our mission giving. Winning souls is the purpose of this church.

The second priority is discipleship training. Making disciples of all nations is the Lord's great command. In a real sense these priorities are a two-in-one priority, for one does not exist without the other. The believers are made disciples, to make more disciples. Through discipleship seminars, expository preaching, Sunday School, leadership training, home Bible study on discipleship, and prayer groups disciples are made.[12]

If we were to look at this ministry in terms of its adherence to both the quantitative and the qualitative criteria discussed earlier, we would first note that it has one of the most diverse congregations I have ever observed. There are fifteen different ethnic groups. The makeup of the body was primarily Asian, Hispanic and Anglo, but over the last year a transition has taken place in the community. More African-Americans and Africans are now living in the immediate area of the church. This church can easily be considered multiethnic along the quantitative dimension.

The qualitative aspect is clearly demonstrated in the formation and structure of the church. Multiethnicity is incorporated into all aspects of the church, including the elders and deacons. Most of the people live within a radius of six miles. The board, made up of elders and deacons, is representative of the congregation but keeps to the biblical criteria for selecting elders and deacons. The celebration and ministry of the church is led and formed by the members of the congregation. My discussions with Oh suggested a great deal of variety in the church, including a significant charismatic, spontaneous component. The pastor allowed others a great deal of room to create ministries suitable for the multiethnicity of the church. No one ethnic group seemed to dominate the life of the church. The church was serious about discipling people and incorporating them into the organism and organization of the body. The pastor did express concern about an illness of the church that he called "koininitis." This illness led the specific ethnic groups to stay together in cliques that excluded others in the congregation. He indicated that this is common in most churches and must be dealt with gently and biblically in order to maintain multiethnicity with biblical integrity.

Oh indicated that reconciliation among the ethnic groups was not necessarily something to approach overtly. As pastor of the church, he was aware of it, especially because of the Los Angeles context and the ongoing racial strife. He sees the formation of diverse groups as part of the reconciliation process. It brings unity without having to make the subject of reconciliation a unique biblical theme.

Oh listed several obstacles that he has encountered in forming a biblical multiethnic church.

1. Tradition. Traditions are very demanding. They are, as he put it, "authoritative and powerful" standards. His fear is that they can become as authoritative as the Scriptures. One illustration reveals Oh's awareness of the dangers of syncretism.

A Cambodian family said to me that they know Buddha is not God. They have accepted the teachings of Jesus and his divinity. Therefore, they were most willing to send their children to Sunday School and church to learn more about Christ. But venerating and honoring Buddha is their tradition. It is the community and national tradition. They want to continue in that way and do not see anything wrong with it. The idea of syncretism of religious beliefs and practices of the multiethnics is one of the greatest problems in the multiethnic ministry. It requires enormous time on the part of the church to teach and present biblical Christianity.[13]

2. *Patterns of thinking.* An aspect of culture that is approved by a particular ethnic group may be offensive to another. An example of this is demonstrating affection in public. This practice is not universal and can be harmful to other members of the body. As a matter of fact, it is taboo in some cultures. How we greet each other is important and cannot be minimized in the multiethnic church. Teaching and learning from one another is crucial. As Oh indicated, "There is a need of constant correction and clarification in mutual communication."[14]

3. *Family clans.* "The influence of the clan is one of the greatest drawbacks in the multiethnic ministry."[15] The clan exercises power over the families, determining what they will all do, in spite of the church. There are no individual votes; the family votes as a unit. The family cannot be held accountable to the church over against the clan. Failure in public is the issue at hand. If one fails and is held accountable, that person is a disgrace and will experience shame. To be accountable when one succeeds or is good at some-

thing is okay. According to Oh, in reference to the multiethnic church, "the concept of accountability, certain patterns of thinking (such as social, economic and political issues) and manners have hardly found room in the minds of the multiethnics."[16]

4. Difficulty in discipleship/leadership training. New believers are often not encouraged by their families to pursue discipleship or leadership training. "Son, don't be too religious. You can skip the church service once in a while. Don't be so fanatic about the church. You are young. Taste the world."[17] The concept of discipleship is foreign to most people coming from other countries. The pastor does everything and is paid to do so. Participation in discipleship programs is most difficult to achieve because of the lack of biblical teaching from the outset of the Christian experience. Also, many have to work two jobs, and many must move quite often to locations near their employment.

5. Redemption and lift. This is a church-growth principle noted by Donald McGavran. Often when people become Christians, they become more stable financially, which allows them to move away from the community they lived in before receiving the Lord in salvation. The gap between their past and present lives can be enormous. Prosperity very often becomes a trap of comfortableness. Maintenance of a new lifestyle can move people away from the church. Rather than giving more to the Lord out of gratitude, they often give less.

These points are important for pastoral staff to bear in mind as they attempt to maintain a multiethnic congregation. I believe that, to one degree or another, this occurs in many of the churches that are seriously and biblically taking on the challenge of multiethnicity. Kraft indicates that the "church should be leading the way in bridging the gap between diverse groups of people. God seems to value diversity, and Christians need to be expressing God's acceptance of ethnic differences."[18]

Church Model: Rock of Our Salvation

This ministry is located in the Austin community of Chicago, which is made up primarily of African-Americans. The pastor of this church is Raleigh Washington. Glen Kehrein, director of Circle Urban Ministries, also has leadership responsibilities at Rock of Our Salvation. This church's numerical growth has leveled off at 150 members, with 400 people attending services.

Washington and Kehrein met under unusual circumstances. Kehrein explained to me that Washington had come from a career in the military. He had been the victim of racism, as whites were not able to accept his advancements over them and forced him to leave the service. Kehrein had been involved in a previous cross-cultural ministry situation that broke apart in the absence of true racial reconciliation. The Lord brought these two hurting men together to develop a deliberate model of racial reconciliation in a community greatly in need of a manifestation of the kingdom of God.

Kehrein indicates that they stumbled into the realization that the kingdom of God and the heart of the gospel have to do with reconciliation. "That's the very nature of the gospel, reconciling us to God, and then it says in 2 Corinthians the fifth chapter that's the ministry . . . reconciling the world to God and to each other."[19] This ministry is described by Kehrein as a bicultural (rather than multiethnic) church. It is concerned primarily with breaking down the walls and initiating healing between the white community and African-Americans. The leaders find this work to be extremely difficult and complicated. Kehrein notes that a multiethnic congregation seems more complicated "because culture drives us apart. Society, essentially, has become very, very good at separating and segregating us, so if we're going to go against the grain, we need to be intentional . . . about reconciliation."[20] When he says that they must work at it, that is reconciliation; they must "work on it to bring black and white folks to the same church and be involved in the same ministry because . . . it will generally not happen by itself."[21]

Kehrein and the pastoral staff agree that presence is not enough. He notes that "churches feel that . . . if . . . there's a presence of another ethnic group, a significant presence in the church, . . . that by its nature [it] makes them [think] . . . they're doing racial reconciliation, and I don't think that's the case."[22] He goes on to say that "until you're dealing with these kinds of issues, . . . [like] power,"[23] you are not doing racial reconciliation. My discussion with Kehrein about reconciliation disclosed his disappointment with the evangelical church. He is a graduate of the Moody Bible Institute and claims to be an evangelical with a noncompromising commitment to the inerrancy of Scripture.

Breaking Down Walls, a book written about the ministry of Washington and Kehrein, lays out eight principles for developing this type of ministry. These principles represent the thinking and ministry of many key leaders. As I studied the multiethnic church in Chicago, I discovered the importance of each of these precepts. Therefore, I have listed them along with my analysis of how I see them at work at Rock of Our Salvation and in other contexts.

1. Commitment to relationship. They believe that it is imperative for us as Christians to cross the cultural boundaries of our comfort zone to meet others in order to break down the barriers and misunderstandings accumulated over the years. Biases and misunderstandings will continue to be part of our worldview unless we get to sit in a context other than our own and listen and learn from others. A key word in building relationships is *effort.* Relationship-building is not easy. Great patience and effort are demanded to go against the stream of the life we have become used to. Today it is much more difficult than ever to build relationships. Rather than making life less complicated and more free, technology, in imposing all kinds of information and demands on us, has made life even more busy and congested.

As my good friend Doug Hall has often pointed out to me, we are not living in the context of primary relationship-building where people interface and talk with each other. That primary sector seems to be missing. In its place is secondary communication, which looks ahead rather than at each other. One rarely meets new acquaintances at the movies or by looking into the computer monitor.

Relationship-building may have become a lost art in the church. The analogy used by the authors of *Breaking Down Walls* is marriage. "When a man and a woman marry, they vow to not quit when the going gets rough ('until death do us part'). That is the kind of commitment needed to accomplish racial reconciliation."[24] We must understand that building relationships brings conflicts. Conflict goes hand in hand with any relationship. The issue is, How do we correct conflict so that the church grows in maturity? Kehrein and Washington discovered this while they were on their "marriage" journey. The passage that became important to them was Philippians 2:2-3.

It doesn't matter what the conflict is. When conflict is seen from a black perspective or a white perspective, the racial dynamic crosses all issues. Assumptions are made, often based on stereotypes about racial attitudes. But if we acknowledge this and commit ourselves to hang in there and work through it, we'll have taken a giant step toward racial reconciliation.[25]

The subject of racial reconciliation was not mentioned very often in my investigation, and certainly conflict resolution was not highlighted. Many Christians seem to want to ignore the conflicts involved in the process because conflict does not speak well of "our ministry." Conflicts are viewed as being personal in nature rather than as being rooted in ethnic and cultural differences; therefore, our solutions may never deal with the root of the problem.

2. Intentionality. This subject came up continually in my discussion with Kehrein. Intentionality was not included in the development of many of the other models that I examined, especially in relationship to personal relational matters in a crosscultural setting. "If we expect it [racial tension] to break down by itself without our being doggedly intentional about it, we're naive."[26] Clearly racial reconciliation will not happen on its own.

Some of the pastors I interviewed expected racial reconciliation to happen as people came together in the same milieu. This does assist the process to a certain extent, but I discovered that people usually prefer to stay in "common waters." They do not like to go beyond the familiar. It seems clear to me that racial reconciliation will not occur if the church is not intentional about it. "These barriers didn't come falling down by accident; Jesus intentionally went out of His way to make a point."[27]

In this model the church creates numerous opportunities for people to gather together for the purpose of learning from each other and building relationships. One of these events was the "Chocolate, Vanilla and Fudge Ripple." This was a meeting designed specifically for interaction on cultural issues and the more intense issues in relation to racial reconciliation. African-Americans get together to discuss their concerns, and the whites do the same in an all-white setting called the "vanilla" meeting. After lunch they all get together to eat fudge ripple ice cream and Oreo cookies as they discuss the issues. In some of these meetings repentance, forgiveness and reconciliation take place.

Another event this church sponsors is a week-long festival of luncheons for seniors, the homeless, and men and women of the community. In the evening they have a tent meeting that is similar to an old-fashioned revival meeting. On Saturday they set up a carnival in the community with a lot of singing and general fun. The groups are brought together by this event and learn about each other in a casual setting.

We need help breaking out of the security of our homogeneous settings and engaging brothers and sisters who are very different from us. We need to be more intentional about building relationships for the sake of bringing justice and harmony into a racially worn and torn society. It is possible to be active in a multiethnic congregation without ever being challenged on the subject of racism and paternalism.

3. *Sincerity.* A great deal of mistrust exists between black people and white people. Kehrein and Washington refer to this as part of the historical reality of the African-American people in the land of their captivity and slavery. They note that even when people do attempt to build relationships with others, the one ingredient usually missing is trust. In order for trust to be included in this process, people must be sincere. This means that the members of the congregation are called to be vulnerable. The synonym for *sincerity* in this case is *vulnerability,* a willingness to open up one's life to others and speak and share honestly about personal life issues.

The mission statement of Rock of Our Salvation falls under the acronym CALLED:

C—Crosscultural Church

A—in the Austin community

L—under the Lordship of Christ

L—building Leaders

E—through Evangelism

D—and making Disciples[28]

This mission statement strongly encourages the matter of building trust in a church where 70 percent are black and 30 percent are white. Such sincerity calls for time, initiative and honesty from all the members. Anyone who wants to join this congregation, after reviewing the mission statement, would have to join with the leaders in a willingness to work toward the goal of reconciliation.

4. Sensitivity. Being sensitive to others is a way in which people display respect. Assumptions are dangerous and often damage the relationship-building process. This goes for both African-Americans and Anglos. Sincerity is the ability to speak honestly about our feelings in a particular situation. It also means that we think highly of persons of all ethnic backgrounds and that we attempt to be sincere by listening to others both verbally and nonverbally.

5. Interdependence. This subject directly confronts the homogeneous unit principle. Both Washington and Kehrein have difficulty with this principle in relationship to unity and solidarity in the body of Christ. All groups, not just African-Americans and whites, tend to separate and to worship among themselves. The question is, Do we need each other? Those who follow the HUP, Afrocentrism or other forms of self-determinism are satisfied with different churches. This amounts to adopting a "separate but equal" stance in our houses of worship. Washington and Kehrein base their ministry on the belief that we do indeed need each other.[29] This point was strongly made in my interview with Kehrein.

The concern for credibility and for modeling of racial reconciliation was made clear. It is important for this church to speak about people needing each other. The leaders need to understand that many in the African-American community may be very hesitant to say that they need white people. Reverend Washington is willing to say that he needs white people because God, as he puts it, has called him to racial reconciliation. This sense of partnership is important if we are to be Christians in a world that is so racially torn. We are not to take sides, but rather to "take over" for the Lord Jesus Christ. The goal of interdependence is to display the unity of the body in the midst of diversity.

6. Sacrifice. The Christian life is one of sacrifice. Sacrifice is not wanting things your way. In crosscultural ministry we are challenged to consider others and their needs ahead of our own. It is a giving up in order to build relationships. This church is diverse socioeconomically as well as culturally, which complicates the task of reconciliation. The process of reconciliation will be a matter of both groups being able to give up, to sacrifice in order to see the Lord receive the glory.

7. Empowerment. This aspect of the process is, for me, the most important. It shows how far we have progressed in the direction of justice. Kehrein and Washington indicate that this is the foundation of the ministry of reconciliation. The two theological themes are repentance and forgiveness. This, for them, is where freedom comes to the body of Christ. "An attitude of repentance empowers the other person—or group, or race—to lay aside anger and blame, and it opens the path to forgiveness."[30] This element of repentance was often lacking in my discussions of the subject of reconciliation with pastors and lay leaders. Too often discussion was more sociological than biblical. The assertions of reconciliation without supporting evidence were disheartening.

8. Call. For Rock of Our Salvation, the calling of the Lord is seen both as a call to reconciliation and as a call to incarnational living as the means to reconciliation. Their basic belief is that all are to be involved in the ministry of reconciliation; on the other hand, because they see racial reconciliation as being possible only within the incarnational setting, they do not believe that all are called to be race reconcilers. I have some difficulty with defining racial reconciliation as a special gift or as a special call. Such terms are too narrow in their implications for how such reconciliation can take place. It allows most people to remain in their zone of comfort without embracing their responsibility to those who are different from them. The incarnational piece is a call to relocate into a poor, minority community. In this case the church is called to justice, and justice must approach the error of racism; however, the whole body, not just those who physically relocate, must answer the call to be witnesses.

Conclusion

Clearly the multiethnic church will take a great deal of work, fasting and prayer. It is a dynamic ministry that depends on the Lord's grace to bring together very diverse people who will eventually begin to appreciate each other and to learn in humility the greatness of our Lord, who brings all nations to himself. Knowing very well that this gathering is (humanly speaking) unnatural, God meets this group of believers in fellowship and reminds them that "where two or three come together in my name, there am I with them" (Mt 18:20).

Small Group Discussion Questions

1. Here you are again faced with definitions. What do you think the importance of definition is to your understanding of multiethnic ministries?

2. Should you, as a group, take on the challenge of developing your own definition in relationship to the MEC? Give it a try and discuss what you learned from this exercise.

3. This chapter introduced the qualitative and quantitative dimensions involved in establishing an MEC. Are those terms useful to you? Why? Describe both categories as they relate to your present small group.

4. The International Bible Church in Los Angeles is a fascinating ministry. Does this ministry seem too far out to be considered as a possible model for you to use in developing a multiethnic small group?

6
MULTIETHNIC LEADERSHIP

*J*OHN PERKINS, IN A 1994 COMMENCEMENT ADDRESS AT WHEATON College, stated,

> Whenever God gets ready to do something in our society, he starts with leaders. God is not a herding God. He's not a mass action God. God is a leadership God. He raises up leaders. He gives those leaders burdens and visions, the leaders apply their ideas to society, and society follows them.[1]

Our examination of the multiethnic church so far strongly suggests that the proper leadership is essential to establishing and maintaining the quantitative and qualitative aspects of the ministry. Leadership determines the future of the multiethnic church. This means that the experiences, training and spiritual maturity of these key individuals will decide the outcome and effectiveness of a multiethnic ministry that is biblically founded and is sociologically aware of the community in which it has decided to serve. But a leader is not a random selection or a product of secular training; a leader is, as Ted Ward reminds us, "one who ministers; a leader *serves* through the gifts of the Holy Spirit, not in terms of prowess, not in terms of accomplishments or acquired knowledge, but in terms of what God is doing through his or her life. Leadership in the church is servanthood."[2] This also means that leaders are evaluated in terms of Scripture. There are several elements in this category of leadership.

The Leader as Pastor

In every case the direction for the MEC process was instituted by the one who acted as the senior pastor. The pastor was the visionary, the one who experienced the initial conviction to move toward establishing a format that would bring diverse people groups together. The pastor also solicited and engaged other pastors to join in this challenge. He or she was the one who "sold" the idea to the congregation and to the staff that would eventually support the development of the MEC. In every one of the cases the pastor of the local congregation was the key figure. None of the models were developed by lay leaders, although these leaders provided very significant assistance to the pastor. The one exception to this rule is The Church In The City, a church in Denver which was started by lay leaders who eventually became the pastors.

I would also point out that in almost all cases the pastor carried the full burden of this process for many years. Few in the congregation (or, in some cases, in the leadership) were as committed or as willing to carry out the call to racial and ethnic sensitivity that leads to reconciliation as the pastor. It is my opinion that an MEC that starts with much joy and commitment can dissolve if it loses this pastor-visionary. The congregation's depth of commitment to the MEC, as well as its understanding of the necessity of the MEC, is often shallow. It needs to become much more involved in the process of developing the ministry for the MEC to provide the living resources for each member.

I encountered this lack of commitment in the pastoral staff of two of the congregations I researched. In these churches the senior pastor, the one who initiated the process, seemed to be the primary person maintaining the commitment to bring healing and justice to the community and the church. The other pastors from different ethnic groups were faithful to the MEC and its meaning to their congregations, but they were also very committed to the homogeneity of their local group. I would venture to say that the homogeneous group is the primary concern for many of the pastors who are leading specific ethnic groups. The reason for this is that the pastors are committed to reaching out to their people. They are comfortable in that context and, predictably, find greater success in it. The homogeneous groups in the multicongregational church operate in a language other than English. Their cultural distinctives are kept intact and, therefore, are not profoundly influenced by the multiethnicity dynamic. On the other hand, the English-speaking congregations are influenced personally and structurally toward change.

The multicongregational church that has several congregations of different ethnic groups serving within the same framework and government and in the same facility becomes a multiethnic church when the second generation of each ethnic group assimilates into the English-speaking congregation. It is to be the ongoing formation of the church. Each language group becomes a "feeder" to the English-speaking congregation. This congregation will experience the issues of multiethnicity more profoundly and will enjoy growth due to this arrangement.

The pastor is the one who keeps a careful eye on the congregation. The pastor is shepherding the flock on the understanding that God has entrusted the congregation to him or her (Acts 20). The pastor's call is not to develop a multiethnic church but rather to enhance the growth of the congregation toward a new humanity founded on Christ and to take on this mission challenge in his or her context. Without biblical pastoring we have self-centered vision that violates the trust God has placed in that individual.

The Leader's Training

Training and education were significant to the success of most of the leaders interviewed. Their educational backgrounds varied from graduate degrees, such as a Ph.D. or a D.Min., to some courses in a Bible college. Most pastors had some form of formal education. The most helpful preparation for ministry seemed to be a blend of theological training and social sciences and was obtained through both formal and informal modes. These leaders had skills in the biblical field that allowed them to be faithful to the task of exegesis and also had abilities to interpret the sociological realities of their communities. Their experiences in multiethnic communities, which often included their upbringing, were very useful. Those who served in foreign missions were accustomed to crosscultural dynamics and found that it was for them the most enjoyable context in which to live and to serve. Some of the pastors grew up in the city and had learned to appreciate the diversity of their communities.

My conclusion is that training for those working in ethnically diverse communities is an essential part of the process of building a multiethnic church. Such training may be found in continuing education programs or in ongoing denominational programs that equip pastors and missionaries. Regardless, the importance of training cannot be minimized. The proper training saves time, helps avoid needless hardships, and promotes the efficient utilization of scarce funds.

Missionaries who leave for a foreign field are trained in anthropology, sociology and missiology and in most cases are expected to have a theological degree (e.g., the M.Div.). They learn a new language prior to departing for the mission field. Similar training must accompany the process of establishing an MEC. Most of this training, as was previously mentioned, takes place on the field while the work is being established. I believe we could alleviate some of the problems and conflicts through a curriculum that covers both theology and the social sciences. I do not see this as an exhaustive program, but rather as one that provides the tools for doing theology and social interpretation. Nor do I see this as a substitute for the spontaneous work of the Holy Spirit. Too often training and education get a "bad rap" as being irrelevant and as quenching the work of the Holy Spirit. I do not believe that this is necessarily true, but certainly it has happened, and in some cases it continues to occur. My concern is that the curriculum for this kind of work be very context-specific.

The Leader's Commitment to the Authority of Scripture

My research determined that the churches relied on Scripture as the authority for the church and life. The Bible was the churches' manual in reference to multiethnicity. The Word of God will build this new humanity, and it must be central to the ministry of multiethnicity. I had only one opportunity to investigate a church where this was not the case, but in all the other situations the Scriptures were fundamental to the establishment of ministry. The pastors were evangelicals who understood the ongoing dialogue that warns the church about the pitfalls of pluralism and multiethnicity. "There is a definite link between pluralism and relativism that is part philosophical and part psychological."[3]

It was also true that differences did make a difference, and that in most cases relativism was not a factor. Reinforcement of tradition and biblical truth were more the rule. The Scriptures were central to the evaluation of the multiethnic church in confessional churches, such as the Presbyterian Church in America, and in churches that held an evangelical commitment. Syncretism was easy to detect and deal with. An example of this was the issue of discipline in the church. In some cultures losing face in front of a congregation or group of leaders is an offense. Yet the agreement among the pastors in the multicongregational church was that Scripture must be the determining factor in dealing with sin and error. The pastors included in this study also evaluated their worship in light of Scripture. Culture should not be the last word in determining how worship is carried out in the church.

The pastors of the multiethnic churches that I evaluated used the biblical text for their positioning, rather than trends and social context. This does not mean that they ignored culture, but rather that the pastors' position on Scripture forced them to do theology in the milieu of a diverse community. This also provided the pastors with an understanding that multiethnicity must have a quantitative dimension that leads them to view justice and the righteousness of Christ as high priorities. The Scriptures led leaders to embrace justice and racial harmony for the sake of enhancing God's kingdom. It was not enough to have diversity; racial reconciliation on a biblical plane had to be implemented.

The Leader's Commitment to Missions

The gospel is good news, not relevant advice. The good news encompasses both evangelism and social involvement. The pastors in this study were concerned about church growth and foreign missions. This was contagious, inspiring the other leaders to reach people for Christ. The community was defined in terms of the unchurched, a community of various religions that needs to know the Lord of the harvest. The description of the community was derived from its spiritual condition as well as social analysis. It was a missiological definition.

The biblical text most often cited was Matthew 28:19-20. The context of mission was their neighborhood, and in their neighborhoods lived diverse peoples who needed to know about Christ's amazing love and acceptance. The church needed to provide this news in the language of the people with sensitivity toward their culture. To accomplish this, some pastors solicited other pastors with skills in the various community languages to join the English congregation in a combined effort to reach the community. This mission focus, in my opinion, is the beginning of the multiethnic church. It happens as an outreach effort in a multiethnic context. A vision to see the multitudes come to Christ is part of the motivation. Another part is recognizing that the church is the continuing incarnation of Christ and that it must claim its parish for the Lord.

Conversion growth in most of these congregations was high, higher even than transfer growth, even though that model of ministry is very appealing, especially to young people under the age of thirty-five. There is a certain excitement in these churches that is generated by their missionary zeal and their cultural diversity. The work of the ministry is being done in a mission context. The congregation is involved in outreach and discipleship, and this makes for a high-energy church that is excited about worship and fellowship. Sunday morning presents the congregation with new Christians who are zealous about their newfound faith in Christ. The combination of missions and new Christians hungry to learn about Christ provides the church with growth and empowerment to continue the work of Christ in a mission context.

One pastor shared with me his view that Christians have no option in the matter of evangelism. If the Lord brings to us people of a different culture, we are again faced with the biblical reality that God is no respecter of persons and that we are to serve the world with God's love and compassion.

Everything that is not under the scrutiny of the Word of God is dangerous. If, because of God's effective grace, a Nigerian, Korean, Chinese or Hispanic is saved, it is the responsibility of that local congregation to bring the new Christian into the fold with joy and celebration of what the Lord has done. Salvation is the work of God; we are but vessels of grace, debtors who are willing to tell the good news to those who will hear. If God has chosen an African-American to come into his family, who am I to reject God's good pleasure?

René Padilla exhorts us,

Whether a person likes it or not, the same act that reconciles one to God simultaneously introduces the person into a community where people find their identity in Jesus Christ rather than in their race, culture, social class, or sex, and are consequently reconciled to one another. The unifier is Jesus Christ and the unifying principle is the "Gospel."[4]

The multiethnic church is only a manifestation of God's grace. Relativism in the church embraces the culture of this country which promotes segregation rather than understanding God's call to care for the multitudes with love and compassion.

The pronouncements of many apologists and philosophers seem to be oblivious of what is happening in the evangelical church as it serves in the city among diverse peoples. The Christology of these churches exalts the name of Christ. God-centered evangelism would bring joy to R. B. Kuiper and Paul Little. Many recent writings on the subject of pluralism and multiculturalism present a one-sided perspective, warning the church of multiculturalism's ability to penetrate the body of Christ, thereby compromising the gospel. This narrow position can do harm by alienating people from those who are on the forefront of warning the church against intellectualism. Who are the ones with the "fat minds"[5] that need correcting? Ministers who have very little concern for or training in missions and crosscultural experience may find themselves unwilling to tackle this work. A congregation that has no interest in a parish concept (because they view the parish as "the world") will also renege on the Lord's contextual provision. We all need to know our mission context. What is yours?

The Leader's Commitment to Spiritual Formation

The multiethnic church experiences in its ministry a tension that is not common in the homogeneous church. The conflicts that arise out of the milieu of diversity present the church with new questions. I discovered that the pastors I interviewed relied heavily on prayer and fasting for the formation of the church and its leaders. The ministry of prayer was well organized. It was as important to the church as any of the regular church meetings that demanded the congregation's attendance. The prayer life of the leaders was nurtured and encouraged, and they were held account-able to a prayerful lifestyle. I also encountered a group of pastors and staff who were very committed to each other and relied on prayer for the development of their unity and love. The fellowship of believers was Christ-centered, and the leaders maintained a po-sition that praying together brought greater harmony to the church than any other activity.

It always seems easier to do something on our own rather than to delegate, and this is true of our role as instruments of God. We resist turning over our concerns to the Lord. Delegating them to the Lord is too time-consuming, and we honestly believe that we can do it more quickly and more efficiently. We are extremely busy and enjoy the complicated life even though we would be hard pressed to admit it. The ministry of multiethnicity is the work of the Lord God through the Holy Spirit. Our ministries are initiated and ignited by the Holy Spirit and must be carried out by God the Holy Spirit. This means that we must devote time and effort to growing in grace as we lay our lives before the Lord.

The breaking down of the barriers between Jew and Gentile, between slave and free, and between male and female could no more be taken for granted in the first century than the breaking of the barriers between black and white, between rich and poor, and between male and female today. But all the New Testament evidence points to an apostolic practice consistent with the aim of forming churches in which God's purpose would become a concrete reality.[6]

Conclusion

These five leadership themes showed themselves in each of the churches evaluated and played an important role in the development of leadership ministering in a pluralistic society. Leadership needs to become more aware of the mission context. It is interesting to note that leaders have difficulty defining their context of mission. They seem to be trying to do missions without a context. In discussing their context, they quickly noted preparation. The context usually stimulates needs and therefore training and education. "How can I be better prepared to serve the Lord in this changing community and world?" This is their question. The reason we have ignored leadership issues, continuing to frame things in the order of the past, is that we have not taken time to read the new signs of the present.

Small Group Discussion Questions

1. Leadership is presented as the most important element in reaching the goal of establishing a multiethnic church or small group. What is your opinion? Explain.

2. This chapter lists the leadership qualities necessary for multiethnic ministry. What would you add to this list as important in working with a diverse group of people?

3. Spiritual formation is extremely important to any ministry. How would you define spiritual formation in light of your tradition and understanding?

4. Evaluate the gifts of your group and determine through discussion how you might best use them in this multiethnic context.

7

PREPARING
THE CHURCH FOR
MULTIETHNIC
TRANSITION

*P*REPARING A CONGREGATION THAT IS BOTH ETHNICALLY AND SOCIO-
economically homogeneous for an ethnic and cultural transition
is not simply a matter of having vision or of missiological stimu-
lation. The transition must be accomplished carefully in order to
help the existing congregation to be open to change, at least in
the initial stages. The element of intentionality is most important.
Everything that we do should be thought through carefully and
open to review. We can identify five elements that are essential to
equipping the congregation for major changes in the structure of
the church.

Studying Community

Be intentional in studying and disclosing demographic information. Studying community, or what some call exegeting community, is not something that comes naturally to people, especially
Christians. We think that the social sciences are for social scien-
tists and that material matters are not spiritual. But lately I have
been pleased to notice a major change in this area: more pastors
are learning their community through the use of sociological tools.
But many remain at a distance from these aids, which could provide a helpful guide as the congregation moves into crosscultural
ministries.

We often leave the congregation in the dark concerning what is
taking place as far as the mission of the church in a transitional
community. The community has changed drastically over a
number of years. We have watched this progression, not knowing
what to do or what this cultural and ethnic transition means. The
leadership has done some demographic work to affirm its suspi-
cions that the community is going through a major change. But
the information it gathers is not provided to the church and is not
interpreted for its members in a way that would allow them to see
the necessity of becoming much more multiethnic as a church, of
reaching out to make the church grow. In some cases this is a life-
and-death situation for the church. The pastor and the church
leaders may be convinced on the basis of this information that the
church will have to take on this challenge, but they are negligent
in disseminating the information more widely than to the leadership. This step must be accomplished with sensitivity, understanding the mindset of the congregation at this point in the history of
the church.

It is a major fault of leadership not to process the community data. It is a mistake to assume that the congregation will not understand the information. It should be presented in a nonthreatening manner that emphasizes the opportunity for missions and a healthy growing and lasting ministry.

James Westgate has written an important article entitled "Transitions and the Urban Church."[1] He identifies six transitions that occur in most communities: (a) generational transitions in which young people replace older members; (b) economic transitions in which people who made major financial contributions to the church have moved; (c) geographical transitions that involve migration patterns in the community; (d) cultural and ethnic transitions (the arrival of different ethnic groups) that demand attention because very often these transitions present the greatest threat to the church; (e) racial transitions that challenge the church with the greatest test of all because they open up some of the racial tensions (racism) that have been kept hidden for so many years; (f) spiritual transitions that apply to the spiritual fervency of the church. In the early days of the church there may have been a warmth and an exciting dynamic in the ministry, whereas the church may now be struggling to discover its identity.

Westgate identifies several key attitudes that are helpful in working through the transitions that we encounter. These attitudes may determine the success of the church's crosscultural move.

Permanence. Our attitude toward permanence is a significant determinant of how we respond to transitions. Cities intensify the frequency and complexity of change. City churches experience the stress of a relatively rapid turnover of people and the need for constant spiritual renewal, in contrast to the entrenchment found in rural and suburban areas. But true security does not depend on being in an unchanging community. Whether a change or a turnover involves an ethnic group or an economic structure, our security is based on the eternal and unchanging God. It is based on the eternal values of God's kingdom (1 Pet 1:17-19; 1 Cor 3:12-13). Our mission is not dependent on a changing community or on changing systems but on the sovereign Lord who knows the beginning from the end.

Denying (out of a feeling of fear) that anything is changing or needs changing results in a failure to plan for a positive and orderly transition. Denominations are a great example of this; they are always late in moving with the Spirit of the Lord. This is what happens in Acts 10 and 11—Peter needs to explain to the Jewish Christians what the Lord is doing, even though the Lord had told them that he would reach out to the Gentile world. If we deny what is happening and do not see the transition as a move of the missionary God, we will have missed a salvific opportunity.

If we perceive the people coming into our community as intruders, robbing the church of its peace and prosperity, we will experience feelings of hostility toward them and will want them to stay away from our community. Again, homogeneity—we have not learned to live in diverse ethnic and racial situations. Feelings of fear and anxiety crop up because we have not learned to live together. In our ministries and local churches we have learned to fear those who are nonwhite, nonaffluent and non-English-speaking. We think of them as inferior and potentially violent. Thus we have come to discredit the gospel and the Lord of the gospel.

Renewal and celebration come when we are willing to relinquish control of our churches to the Head of the church, the Lord Jesus Christ. We must surrender our attitudes, customs, methods and power to the lordship of Christ. The unchanging God is the very one who brings about change. God turns people around completely—from death to life. God changes carnality to Christlikeness. When we welcome change, we unleash the Holy Spirit and our creative energies. This change is from the top to the bottom of structure. This means power delegation and trust.

Property. What is our view of property? Middle-class Americans are taught that property is almost sacred. We value it for the control. An unquenchable hunger for power and self-promotion drives us to consume beyond the level of physical need. We neglect developing a biblical understanding of property because theologians are middle class and do not necessarily welcome the results of their findings.[2] This theology of property and possessions may emerge from Third World theologians. How do we view our buildings and property? Who really owns them—do we or does God? Buildings here in America are signs of success. And property is likely to be valued over persons in our ministries. If we see God as the owner of all, we will be more likely to be open to multiethnic ministries that permit other ethnic groups to use the facilities. Such a view of property will open our facilities for community use as well. Finally, it will open our minds to think of alternative models for ministry. The buildings we choose should have multiple uses and low overhead.

Persons. What people mean to us or how we attribute value to people is an important aspect of being open to a multiethnic transition. Too often those who are nonwhite, nonmale, noneducated, nonaffluent, nonyoung and nonbeautiful are kept outside the gate. Mother Teresa calls them the social lepers of our society. If we follow the secular approach of devaluing people, we will (a) minimize outreach by being selective; (b) minimize leadership by selecting only those whom society accepts; (c) minimize meeting needs of those considered "outside-the-gate" people; (d) view the community and our congregation as "us versus them"; and (e) give leftovers to those who are different in determining the use and scheduling of facilities.

Scripture opposes this. We find in 1 Samuel 16:7 that "man looks at the outward appearance, but the LORD looks at the heart." Jesus reached out to the Samaritans. Peter and Paul reached out to the Gentiles. Those who judge will be judged. Such judges dishonor the creation mandate and fail to understand humankind as bearing the image of God.

Power. Craig Ellison defines power as "the ability to influence others in a desired way by the control of tangible or intangible resources. In its rawest terms, power is the ability to get others to do what you want them to."[3] The church also is a place where power is sought and is exercised. In most churches the configuration of power—the people who have the power and the reasons they have it—is very similar to that in the secular world. Rather than power being a matter of spirituality, it is a matter of abilities reflecting qualities other than spirituality. Church leadership, like all leadership that is Christian, must lay aside the things of the world and listen for the voice of the Lord. Secular leadership spends much time in talk and great energy in debate. Spiritual leadership spends much time in prayer and great energy in obeying the Lord.

Purpose. The church and its individual believers can be egocentric or "all-o-centric." Egocentrism focuses on self and is very inward; the egocentic church focuses primarily on bringing comfort to its members. "All-o-centrism" looks to the needs of others, particularly those outside the church. It is mission-oriented. Inward-looking churches tend to be passive and are reactive in the face of transition. This quality makes them likely to resist transitions.

Biblical Justice and Multiethnicity

Be intentional in teaching the church biblical justice and multi-ethnicity. There is such a lack of teaching in this area that many congregations have not been exposed to God's concern for immigrants, people of diverse backgrounds, the poor and the matter of reconciliation on the horizontal plane. Leaving it up to Christians to be Christian without teaching them the Word is a major slip. The Bible must play a major role in the process of transition since it is transformational and will accomplish much. It is not enough to acknowledge the Scriptures simply as God's Word to us about the issues of this day and age.

Individualism and Solidarity

Be intentional in providing examples from biblical and church history that affirm that we are not the first to take on the challenge of multiethnic ministries. God has done it in the past and will continue to do so in the present. As Padilla notes,

> Throughout the entire New Testament the oneness of the people of God as a oneness that transcends all outward distinctions is taken for granted. . . . The Bible knows nothing of the human being as an individual in isolation; it knows only of a person as a *related* being, a person in relation to other people. . . . Accordingly, the church is viewed in the New Testament as the solidarity that has been created in Jesus Christ and that stands in contrast with the old humanity represented by Adam.[4]

This biblical theme needs to be unfolded to our congregations. The teaching of the church needs to reflect on the direction that we have taken in the past and that we need to be taking for the future. Some knowledge about the history of the people of God in regard to multiethnicity will be of great benefit.

History of the Church

Be intentional in teaching the church's history. We will be surprised to learn that in many denominations the church has traveled backward over the last hundred years. We often assume that we have moved forward, that the issues we face are new, and that our forefathers knew nothing of this diverse and complicated society. It is amazing that many churches in the past, such as the Nazarene, Methodist and Reformed denominations, had a greater understanding of the needs of the poor and of multiethnicity than many of our contemporaries. Going back to tradition may serve the church well. Tradition can provide affirmation to a church that wants to make major transitions. Mission in the nineteenth and early twentieth centuries had problems, but it also invented a wheel that might be much more biblical than we expect.

Pros and Cons of Multiethnicity

Be intentional about practical aspects of multiethnicity. We need to provide the church with information that discloses both sides of the coin. There are pros and cons to multiethnicity, and we must be diligent to share the whole picture. We need to know what we will have to give up and what we will have to gain. There is going to be a loss when we contextualize, but there is also going to be a gain. Both of these dimensions need to be reviewed. This kind of honesty will pay major dividends.

It is imperative that we explore areas pertaining to crosscultural conflicts and how to resolve them. The social sciences are a tremendous benefit to us in doing a sociology of the church. They will help us to understand ourselves as well as the people we are learning to live with. We need to establish goals for ourselves, and they must be measurable. These goals will be propitious because

they will provide direction for the church. Visits to other multiethnic or multicongregational churches are helpful. Visit other
churches in your area to see what the Lord is doing in other
congregations. On-site visits are exciting and stimulate questions
and genuine commitment.

Hold debriefing sessions with the congregation and the leaders,
allowing them opportunities to share their concerns and frustra-
tions. These times together provide some of the most valuable
aspects of the training program. There is no particular time require-
ment; it all depends on how long it takes for any congregation to
get hold of the process. The debriefing should continue as the
initial stages move ahead. This is when the leaders and the congregation may say, "We didn't know it would be like this." Racism
needs to be dealt with, but this is difficult for many to discern. Few
see themselves as racist, when in reality many are. How to get them
to see their sin and the opportunity for healing and growth will
be a matter of prayer, sharing the Word and loving confrontation
as things progress. To avoid confronting racism is to allow the
bomb to explode at a time when people are coming to the church
with the desires of ownership and mutual love.

Join with other congregations that are of a different ethnic
makeup to have combined worship and fellowship times. This is
often considered a token experience, but I believe it leads to better
understanding and honest discussion. This aspect of training is
important and will be valuable if there is time for debriefing.

The ideal situation is one in which a pastor-mentor, particularly
the senior pastor, is involved with the leadership. The mentor
should have some experience with the multiethnic church or the
multicongregational church model. This mentor is like a coach
who comes alongside the congregation and provides certain in-

sights that help the church work through the rough spots. This is a must for denominations such as the Nazarenes that are deliberately establishing multiethnic churches. The mentors in the larger church structures are excellent resources for more efficient new church start-ups.

The pastor(s) or leaders must be careful not to make too many assumptions that the others are on board with this process. The truth of the matter is that few understand what is happening, and their agreement and commitment are shallow at the outset. They will need more information and training in order to achieve a growing and mature awareness of what the Lord is doing. Being intentional in what we do will enhance the process of developing a multiethnic church. Avoid leaving things to chance.

Another important factor is church discipline. Because of the many issues that arise in the multiethnic church, the one universal principle that must speak to all issues, whether cultural or not, is Scripture. When discipline is active in the church, it manifests itself often as a means of God's grace to the church. Charles and Marguerite Kraft state, "We need to understand that there is a difference between God's *absolute* reality and the *cultural relative* reality around us. God is absolute, beyond relativity, and he has absolute standards that all people, everywhere, are accountable for. He is, therefore, beyond and outside of any culture, neither endorsing nor condemning any cultural system in its totality."[5]

The pastors should be individuals who understand very well the teaching on repentance and forgiveness, persons of humility who know that the ministry entrusted to them is the work and the grace of the Lord. There is, especially in the multicongregational church, a strong commitment to accountability to each other. No one person is left to a superior position; all are to be held accountable to the others. Submission to one another seems to be the dominant theological paradigm. The pastors understand that the ministry of the church is supernatural and depends on leaders who are committed to a life of prayer and submission. This quality is something that comes out of experience and theological reflection. Those who have pastored come quickly to the understanding that holiness and morality are essential for any ministry ordained by the sovereign Lord.

Conclusion

As I asked pastors questions about principles in developing the MEC, they often expressed regret that this subject had not been presented to them at the outset of their ministries as young pastors and missionaries. I see in this an encouragement to press on with the concept of mentoring, not only for new pastors but also for those who have come to realize the complexity of their ministry.

There is much that must be done in equipping the pastor-leader who is taking on this challenge of the MEC. The pastor is the key component to the success of the ministry in an ethnically diverse community, especially in the initial stages. The intentionality of the church cannot be stressed any more than I have in this chapter. It is an error to allow so much of the ministry to go on without careful consideration of all the particulars that must be included in the process of developing multiethnic ministries. This does not mean that we cannot allow for spontaneity; when we have done our homework, we will actually find more of the kind of fluidity that most of us enjoy.

Small Group Discussion Questions

1. Transitions are always difficult to understand and to accept.

Describe transitions that you have experienced. How did you handle this change as a Christian?

2. Do you recall any transitional experiences in your local church? Share as many of them as you can remember. Were any of them caused by community transitions? How have community changes affected the church?

3. Why are transitions difficult to handle either on a personal level or in a church situation?

4. How should Christians view transitions? Do you have any biblical examples of transitions?

8

BUILDING A NEW
HUMANITY

---

*T*HE CHURCH'S TASK IS NEITHER TO DESTROY NOR TO MAINTAIN ethnic identities but to replace them with a new identity in Christ that is more foundational than earthly identities.[1]

Maintaining the multiethnic church is not the goal of the church that has committed itself to racial reconciliation and justice. If there is a concern for qualitative growth in the multiethnic, multicongregational church, structural change will occur. The church will move toward fulfilling the Word of God and toward applying Scripture to developing a new humanity in Christ. The purpose of maintaining the multiethnic church is to establish a church that is committed to seeing Christ reign among his people and to establishing a people of God who are united in their diversity. "Here—in the corporate new human, in the new homogeneous unit that has been brought into being in Jesus Christ—the only thing that matters is that 'Christ is all and in all.' Those who have been baptized 'into one body' (1 Cor 12:13) are members of a community in which the differences that separate people in the world have become obsolete."[2]

Biblical Foundation for Multiethnic Church Development

Mark Oh notes that models of ministry such as the multiethnic church are tested "on the basis of biblical and theological foundations."[3] He makes six biblical assumptions that are essential for the foundation of a multiethnic church. These assumptions formed the basis of his church. The first assumption is the Great Commission, which calls everyone to reach out to "all ethnics."[4] To Pastor Oh this means that the Great Commission calls every Christian to obedience in the fulfillment of Matthew 28:19-20. The African-American should be reaching out to Asians, and Hispanics should be sharing the gospel with African-Americans. This assumption leaves no room for neglecting people because they are of different ethnicity and color. Not only should Christians be reaching all people, they should also be serving together, since they are brothers and sisters.

Galatians 3:28 contains the second assumption. Oh holds that there should be no personal distinctions in the body of Christ because we are one in Christ. This aspect is fundamental to establishing a multiethnic church that meets together in one sanctuary with one language, but with many distinct cultures. The third assumption is found in Galatians 3:29. The fact that we are all Abraham's offspring, biblically as well as in reality, is great motivation for the multiethnic church. The passage that brings the church to consider this model further is Ephesians 2:14-15, 19. This passage is extremely important for the fourth assumption in that it abolishes ethnocentrism—we are now a new humanity. "The reconciliation was achieved through the death of Christ on the cross by which He removed the barrier existing between God and people, between Jews and Gentiles."[5]

The fifth assumption is based in Paul's declaration in Colossians 3:9-11 that we are no longer living in the old self and have put on the new self. This new self is "Christ culture."[6] Cultural and social distinctions are removed. This, as Oh states, is the true possibility for the multiethnic church. Oh's final assumption in establishing a biblical foundation for the multiethnic church is found in 1 John 4:7. We are all God's children, and we must love each other.

For clarification of these points we should pay heed to what Pastor Oh has to say about Christ culture.

> Through the Christ culture I believe that a multiethnic church can be possible. Christ culture can be placed above other cultures in the ministry. I do not mean, however, that one's culture ought to be abandoned or completely disregarded. I do mean that one's attitudes, values, and ways of behaving can be changed in view of the excellencies of Christ and after His attitudes, values, and conduct as revealed in Scripture.[7]

During my interview with Glen Kehrein from Rock of Our Salvation Church in Chicago he reiterated some material from a book that he and Pastor Washington coauthored about aspects foundational to their ministry. He indicated that reconciliation was a priority of the church. The biblical reasons for this are outlined in their book.[8] They note that "Christ made it a priority" in Ephesians 2:14-15. In using this passage, Kehrein and Washington refer to what Paul considered the historic alienation between Jews and Gentiles. The conflict between Jews and Gentiles in Ephesus was met and resolved with love and compassion. "Paul made the bottom line abundantly clear: Christ's purpose was to bring the two together, creating 'one new [people]' in the body of Christ."[9] They go on to assert that reconciliation was also a priority of the apostle Paul. "In writing to the Colossian church, he described the Christian's new being as undergoing 'a renewal in which there is no distinction between Greek and Jew, circumcised and uncircumcised, barbarian, Scythian, slave and freeman, but Christ is all, and in all' (Colossians 3:11)."[10]

They conclude with their third point that the theological foundation of our faith is reconciliation. "When our relationship with God was broken, God brought us back—reconciled us—to Himself through a personal relationship with His Son and our Savior, Jesus Christ."[11] This section of Scripture was brought to the forefront of many discussions as the reason for the church to pursue reconciliation. It was also clear to many of the pastors that reconciliation has been neglected on both the vertical and the horizontal planes.

Three of the pastors interviewed indicated that their churches were motivated primarily by their understanding of biblical texts that speak to the subject of strangers in our country (Ex 12:49; Lev 24:22; Mt 25:35; Heb 13:2). This was then applied to refugees and new immigrants coming into this country and to the church's commitment to compassion and love. This understanding of Scripture led to reaching out and thus to the formation of multicultural ministry.

Some of the other models were moved by a mission context and by the necessity of developing ministries that meet the needs of the community. The churches that were intentional about multiethnicity and reconciliation had a primary concern for the African-American community and for ongoing oppression in this country and in the evangelical church. They chose to be different and, in pursuing their understanding of Scripture, as they put it, to be on the side of God. The reading of Scripture and of the social context gave way to a ministry that made racial and ethnic reconciliation a primary focus.

Reconciliation: An Edict for the Local Church

My research showed that churches tended to resist formulating a theological declaration that states the church's commitment to racial and ethnic relationships, for various reasons. First, the churches expected a professional, the theologian at a particular seminary, to do this work. They did not see this work as the responsibility of the local church. Where there was a denominational affiliation, the denomination expected its seminary to come up with a statement for the whole church.

Second, there was a lack of confidence in the churches' ability to participate in theological discussions and formulations. The churches were not accustomed to working through issues theologically. They do ministry, and seminaries do theological work and reflection. However, I believe that it is important for the local church to take on the task of reviewing theological positions and writing out its own commitments.

We are reminded that all of us are set apart with the mark of God as God's image bearers (Gen 1:26). There is no such thing as a superior human being (Ps 8:4-6). All of us share the same parents—Adam and Eve (Gen 3:20)—and the same condition of life— sinfulness and fallenness (Gen 2:17; 3:23; Rom 6:19). Our biblical position for the church in matters of unity is stated in 1 Corinthians 12:12-13, Ephesians 4:12-13 and numerous other passages. We are one only because of our common redemption in Christ. The shed blood of Christ is what it takes to belong. Diversity, not sameness, is the means by which God brings us to unity, yet we have been groomed by the church and its behavior to understand belonging as a condition of sameness. God has given diversity a special place in his economy. There is divine reason in diversity.

Steps Toward Establishing the New Humanity

There are a number of practical steps that a church can take to move itself toward becoming a church that focuses on the new humanity in Christ.

1. Declare in written form the biblical position of the church on this matter of unity in diversity. We often write out our theological position on the basic tenets of the faith, and then we stop with that. It is imperative to spell out our theological position on the subject of reconciliation and of building a people of God who adhere to the principles of the new humanity in Christ. This theological position, which becomes part of the church's life and ministry, will enhance the members in building each other up toward this mark. If the church does not spell out its position, it will always be in question and will disturb the members of the church rather than elicit their faithful support. This document can also be used as a tool for teaching those who are coming into the church and for helping them understand the position the church has taken in reference to community ministry, particularly to the various ethnic groups located within the parameters of the parish.

2. Develop a mission statement that will assist the church in its focus to do ministry that is effectual in the context of a multiethnic community. The mission statement provides the church with practical and contextual direction. It specifies how theology functions in the context of the local church. The mission statement is the tension that holds the local church and its ministry accountable.

3. Develop a philosophy of ministry that will put the mission statement into action. This philosophy of ministry will be dynamic. It will undergo adjustments, especially as the context in which the local church does ministry changes. The philosophy of ministry is dependent on the universal principles of Scripture and on the contextual realities of the church and community. All of these elements interact with each other and flesh out the mission statement. People change and communities go through transitions. This means that the philosophy of ministry statement needs periodic reevaluation. The interaction between the universal principles in God's Word and the doctrine of the church will extend into the community and the people being served. The universal principles will not change, but the contextual principles will; therefore, ministries will have to be altered.

4. Involve multiethnic leaders in the process. Multiethnic leadership must be involved actively in the initial developmental stages of the multiethnic church. It is important for the pastor to plan ahead both to identify and to train emerging leaders. Some who are now recent converts may grow spiritually and come to provide the church with strong biblical leadership in the future. Installing elders and deacons who represent the various ethnic groups will help the church move in the biblical direction of establishing a ministry that directs its attention to the new humanity. This does not in any way mean that we compromise our biblical position concerning leadership qualifications. What it does mean is that the church must prepare all of its leaders to fulfill the biblical requirements for elders and deacons. I would suggest a special training track for elders and deacons. This would assist the church in establishing fair representation of the makeup of the church as well as in complying with Scripture in matters of authority over the church. This was clearly exhibited in the First Baptist Church of Flushing. God had provided leaders to guide the church into their biblical mandate of creating a new humanity in Christ under the leadership of the Holy Spirit. The three pastors met regularly with all current and emerging leaders in order to train them to participate in the development of the church's ministry.

5. The church must be deliberate in determining how to resolve conflicts. How do we deal with the inevitable cultural, personal and institutional conflicts? Volumes have been written on this subject, but there are six points that I believe to be especially important in terms of assisting the church when conflict arises.

First, the pastor must be involved in the initial stages of conflict resolution. In many cultures the pastor is the head of the clan, the leader of the tribe who is highly respected and is expected to be the one who solves problems and brings healing. The pastor is called upon for all things. But this complete reliance on the pastor can cause his ministry to become seriously overextended. Many of the pastors with whom I visited wrestled with this subject and looked for ways to wean members from this tradition, which they brought from their native lands. However, attacking tradition at the outset is extremely dangerous. Teaching the Word is crucial in encouraging individuals and families to develop a more biblical lifestyle, eventually allowing for fully functioning elders and deacons. It is also important to promote an understanding of the priesthood of believers as well as the utilization of the gifts of the Holy Spirit by all members of the church. This will take time, however, so it is vital not to delegate the problem to another member of the church until the process of teaching and sanctification becomes apparent. Be patient! The pastor may be assisted by someone who has counseling skills, but that person should not become a substitute for the role and the position of the pastor. I have yet to find a multiethnic church in which the pastor has been able to function as a facilitator rather than as a leader who takes charge of the issues of the church.

Second, the pastor should be trained to distinguish between conflict that is cultural in nature and conflict that is personal and institutional. Identifying the issues correctly will help in prescribing the right biblical solution.

Third, the church should recognize that cultural and personal conflicts will arise in the saintliest of congregations. Teaching and sharing on this subject could be conducted in a Sunday-school class, using case studies as a springboard for healthy discussion. This kind of approach will promote the prevention of conflict as well as search for solutions to it.

Fourth, the church should have opportunities to share its concerns openly. This was done in Raleigh Washington's church, Rock of Our Salvation. Members get together in small, homogeneous groups and then move to a larger, more heterogeneous setting. This will assure the congregation that the leadership and others are hearing their concerns and that help is on the way.

Fifth, the church should bring in some members of local ministries that have experienced success with diversity. The church should also assign reading materials that help people see the fullness of what the Lord is doing in other ministries. Most of these books share their stories without glossing over their problems. They can be very helpful.

Finally, multiethnic small groups should be established. The small group provides the dynamic for ongoing healthy relationships, which, in turn, assist the church as a whole in the continuing work of seeing itself growing in diversity and moving toward a more biblical stand and toward the goal of creating a new humanity in Christ.

The small group is a microcosm of the church as a dynamic organism. The small group may help the church maintain "separate but equal" arrangements. Specific ethnic groups meet separately but join together for activities at particular times of the year. The group may decide to move toward the assimilationist model, which invites people of diversity to join the group as long as they conform to the dominant group. It may have a diversity of people yet continue to function as a homogeneous group. The integrative model seeks integration of the various ethnic groups. It allows the diversity presented by the various groups, but the group's operating format is governed by a dominant group. This model may seem to be moving in the right direction, but it is similar to the assimilationist group. It seems to have good intentions, but power remains in the hands of one segment of the group.

The group that will help the church move in the right direction is the *new humanity* group, which does not represent the various ethnic groups but involves all the different ethnicities in establishing and forming the small group. This proceeds in the direction of Ephesians 2:11-22. The new humanity small group needs to be as intentional as the larger church. Diversity and biblical clarity must inform the goals of the small group. The group should not move ahead without full input from the entire group. Too often pragmatism and expedience turn out to be the goal. This will not do. Time must not be allowed to control our commitment. We must be willing to wait until the whole group can participate mutually. When pragmatism takes over, the group starts to move ahead without some of the members and thus falls into one of the other categories, such as the integrative model. Remember, if some group members (for example, some Hispanics) are unable to use the English language, then English cannot be the common language for the whole group, and the group will have to explore different ways in which to function.

The issue of how to make the best use of time inevitably produces tension, but we need to be willing to work toward a more biblical position. The small group provides for relationship-building, even in regard to the most tense issues. If the small group can learn to deal with some of the distinctiveness issues that are fleshed out as the group functions, it will bring strength to the church. Here is where reconciliation is inaugurated.

In order to display the new humanity successfully, the small group must develop a new pattern of thinking. This new pattern can be summarized in terms of process, change, evaluation and the body of Christ.

Think process. It will take time to move into what the group has envisioned. Here is where endurance is tested. Here is where paternalism, or even racism, may show its ugly head. The process is extremely important, and things may not go as quickly as many would like.

Think change. Change is constant, whether we see it or not. Do not be intimidated by constant change. Most of us like things to happen quickly but remain fixed after that. The small group that is committed to the new humanity must be intentional and must wait on the process that the Lord provides. It also must know that there will be multiple changes that will make people feel uncomfortable and irresponsible.

Think evaluation. Intentionality assumes evaluation. We need to evaluate in order to see how far into the process we are and how well we are doing in reference to the goals of the group. The tendency of any living organism is to revert to old and familiar patterns.

Think body of Christ. The whole group must be involved in the process. Too often the "leader" is the initiator and provides the solutions to all the needs of the group. Do not let that happen. All must share in the group process. Keep in mind that the group was able to answer the question, Why have a multiethnic group? The answer to this question might have included enriching our lives by learning from others, assisting other people who are different from us in making a meaningful contribution to their community, learning how to be inclusive in a pluralistic society, working on biblical reconciliation, or helping in the development of a multiethnic church. All of these possible goals are general, and the group must decide on its particular goals. Many goals involve an *inward* direction, which means that we are growing together and maturing in the grace of God. Others involve an *inward-outward* direction. This primarily deals with reaching out to those within the family of God who are different. This moves us out of our comfort zone and places us in a position of learning and growing both within and without. "I am learning how to depend on others." Finally, some goals involve an *outward* direction. This is more missiological and involves reaching out to those in the community who may be unchurched and may not be Christians.

In 1 Corinthians 2:1-12 we see some of the signs of what a small group's attitude should be if it wants to display the new humanity.

Verse 1: Humility. Modern American nationalism portrays the United States as being superior and powerful—more powerful than any other country. We have all the right stuff, we are great, and we need no one. But this should not be our attitude. Paul enjoyed high status in the Jewish community and was trained to be eloquent. But he never imposed that on anyone. We, in turn, should lay aside our natural desire for recognition and imitate the attitude of Christ, who laid down everything, including his life, for the sake of others.

Verse 2: Centrality of Christ. Christ is central to all that we do. The most important aspect of this gathering is to know Christ and him crucified. It is God's redemptive life and death that permeates the group. It is not culture or some sort of sociological dimension that is at hand but rather all cultures knowing the Redeemer and his wonderful grace. It is the centrality of the group, Christ, that tells us about his redemptive love for all the nations. It is the Christ that brings us together in spirituality and humility.

Verse 3: Honesty. We are prone to hide in fear of being cast out due to our inability of always having to understand others. The honesty of the group will determine how the group will endure the many challenges before it and the process that will keep the relationships intact.

Verse 4: Dependence on God. We are probably more apt to trust our abilities and insights than to lean on the presence of the Holy Spirit. God will take our weaknesses and frailties and use them for his glory.

Verses 5 and 16: Confidence in God (imputation). We have the mind of Christ. We should use all the resources available to us, meaning that we utilize the mind that God has given us. We must think Christianly in the process of developing the group. Remember that the Lord has called us to be the new humanity in Christ.

Very often we are not aware of cultural norms that are operative daily. When we are deprived of some of the norms that keep us safe and comfortable in our regular routine, we can become irritated and possibly even bitter. We usually respond to things automatically; now we are asked to exercise a thinking process rather than rely on long-standing patterns. It is like entering a new, strange environment in which nothing is familiar. We must ask questions, listen to others for interpretation, and sit and ponder before we go on. We do not always appreciate having to think through responses, and we try to return to automatic responses as soon as possible. But this must not happen in the multiethnic small group. Give consideration to the following three suggestions: (a) Recognize that you have a culture and that you must understand your own culture. Culture is dynamic and changes over the years, so some acculturation is going on always. (b) Recognize that everyone has a culture, regardless of their social status. As we move up the social scale, we begin to identify ourselves in terms of our economic status, leaving our cultural identity behind. (c) Recognize that we are incapable of divorcing ourselves from our culture. We are not able to become supracultural, going beyond our culture and becoming free of any culture.

This book is not intended to unravel all the elements of a multiethnic group, but to demonstrate that the multiethnic small group is essential for the development of healthy relationships in a dynamic and growing multiethnic church. Maintaining the multiethnic church (and the multicongregational church) is a biblical task that requires the church to search for the divine purpose of diversity in the body of Christ that is instituted by the Lord and to allow the Holy Spirit to create a new humanity in the context of a multiethnic community.

Conclusion

I hope you have caught the essence of this chapter. Our goal as

Christians is to glorify God in all that we do. Whether we establish a multiethnic church or a multicongregational church, the goal is the same—to yield to the lordship of Christ and allow the God of all nations to form the culture of the cross, the new humanity in Christ.

Small Group Discussion Questions

1. Discuss Paul Hiebert's statement quoted at the outset of this chapter. What do you make of it?

2. What biblical framework best suits your group as to the multiethnic church? Which Scriptures do you believe to be beneficial in assisting the multiethnic church to reach its goal?

3. What is your definition of racial reconciliation?

4. Have you ever experienced racism, ethnocentrism or segregation? What were your feelings either as the person excluded or as a friend of one who was excluded?

9

DO YOUR
HOMEWORK!

━━━━━━━

*P*ROBABLY THE LAST THING YOU WANT TO HEAR IS: DO YOUR HOME-
work! There is a lot of hard work before us, and we may be tempted
to delegate it to someone else. I have provided you with a guide
on how to start developing a church in a multiethnic context. A
few more things need to be considered.

The goal in all of this work is to see the Lord build a new
humanity that confronts the spirit of this age and disrobes its
evilness. Justice must flow like a river (Amos 5:24) through the life
of the church. Multiculturalism and inclusivism are not ends in
themselves. Above all, we must come to grips with the biblical
mandate of justice. In our forward progress we must not be moved
by our compassion alone but also by the compassion and the love
of Christ for those whom we call strangers and foreigners in the
land. "If one part suffers, every part suffers with it; if one part is

honored, every part rejoices with it" (1 Cor 12:26). God is calling us to a new order of life, and this demands transformation, a radical biblical change.

Our homework includes biblical studies that will enhance our understanding of pluralism without compromising the concerns of Christ and world evangelization. "Am I now trying to win the approval of men, or of God?" (Gal 1:10). The subject of justice has been too often left for others to do and to think about as if we had no responsibilities in the matter. We must again visit the Scriptures, which show that justice was a priority to the Lord, not a secondary concern.

Our homework also entails training leadership that lives out the gospel incarnationally in this massive, changing society. Leadership makes things go. It sets the pace and often the procedure for others to follow. The training of leaders is extremely important, especially when they are confirmed in their calling to serve the Lord in this unique ministry and context. Short-circuiting this component will bring disaster upon the church. There is no substitute for training leaders who will be doing multicultural ministry.

Our homework will utilize the social sciences to analyze your community or, as I like to call it, your mission context. In this book I have coached you on the importance of demographics, anthropology and contextualization. This work of knowing your community is an ongoing task that helps the church to do ministry more effectively. It is a labor that is not highly esteemed by evangelicals, but I encourage you to make the greatest use of these skills and of information gathering that you can. Beginning to make use of the social sciences is like being introduced to the computer when we have been reluctant to try technical methods.

Once we become familiar with the computer, we wonder how in the world we ever lived without one. This will also be your experience in regard to the use of the social sciences.

Most of all, our homework includes reflection, meditation and prayer. In this volume we talked lightly about the subject of contemplation. Those who understand contemplation know that contemplation and effective missions are inseparable. Prayer sustains and energizes the multiethnic church as much as it does any Christian ministry. I am sure you are saying, "I know this is true, but I find it difficult to do." This lays before us a commitment, a discipline, that will bring us fruit and peace from the words and practices of Christ.

Finally, our homework is to evaluate our ministries. Too often we are afraid to examine how things are going and prefer to leave our progress to chance. But I suggest that ongoing evaluation of what we are doing should be as much a part of our endeavor as prayer. Evaluation keeps us praying for wisdom. It also alerts us to any need for changes, which if made early on might avoid future damage. René Padilla finds some encouragement in Galatians 3:28.

No one would, on the basis of this passage, suggest that Gentiles have to become Jews, females have to become males, and slaves have to become free in order to share in the blessings of the gospel. But, no justice is done to the text unless it is taken to mean that in Jesus Christ a new reality has come into being . . . a unity based on faith in Him, in which membership is in no way dependent upon race, social status, or sex. No mere "spiritual" unity, but a concrete community made up of Jews and Gentiles, slave and free, men and women, all of them as equal members of the Christ-solidarity—that is the thrust of the passage. And, as Donald Guthrie puts it, "Paul is not expressing a hope, but a fact."[1]

The multiethnic global reality inevitably will overtake Christian organizations. We must start thinking anticipatorily as we discern the signs of the future so that we can minister joyfully, not defensively, as we embark on a mission that we have received from the Lord. One day we will all be singing together the praises of our Lord (Rev 5:13).

Small Group Discussion Questions

1. Is it possible for your small group to consider becoming a multiethnic small group within your local church? This should be the intentional result of recognizing that there are numerous people from different communities and countries in your church.

2. What is your task as a small group, if you decide to accept this challenge? Decide on the first step.

3. Are you encouraged to begin such a move? This is a time to speak freely of your fears and misgivings.

4. Does this book help you with the suggested homework assignments? How do you plan to share the responsibilities?

Appendix

Definitions of a Multiethnic Church

Paul Hiebert of Trinity Evangelical Divinity School:

> [A multiethnic church is] a church in which there is (1) an attitude and practice of accepting people of all ethnic, class and national origins as equal and fully participating members and ministers in the fellowship of the church; and (2) the manifestation of this attitude and practice by the involvement of people from different ethnic, social and national communities as members in the church.[1]

Michael Mata of the School of Theology at Claremont:

> [A multiethnic church understands that the manifestation of] significant presence is that there is to the observer notable diversity in the congregation. There exists a qualitative aspect to the notion of a multiethnic congregation. The percentage breakdown of ethnic groups within a congregation may reveal a dominant group, but the sense is that overall the congregation is diverse; it cannot be merely labeled as a white/Anglo, Hispanic or Asian church. . . . The environment of a "truly" multiethnic congregation affirms the diversity of the congregation. For example, room decor, signage, bulletin boards, etc. would reveal a diverse congregation even if you didn't see the people.[2]

Roger Greenway of Calvin Seminary:

> A multiethnic congregation obviously is composed of members of different ethnic backgrounds. But more than that, a true [multiethnic] congregation blends distinctive elements of various ethnic traditions in such a way that no single tradition predominates or suppresses the

others. Nor is the outcome such an "osterized" mixture that nobody can tell one element from another.[3]

Hoover Wong of Fuller Seminary:

[A multiethnic church combines] two distinct monocultural, monolingual groups interacting as one congregation with an agreed, common third culture and language, for example, Western English. . . . [This is] not to be confused with two distinct cultures meeting side by side on one property, sharing facilities, maintaining a parallel society and ministries.[4]

Robert Lupton of Atlanta:

[A multiethnic church is] one that intentionally recruits/embraces diversity and works out structures that assure diversity to continue within the congregation. I do not consider a predominantly single-ethnic congregation that has a few assorted others as members a multiethnic church.[5]

Notes

Foreword
[1]Vincent Bacote, "When Will There Be Room in the Inn? Minorities and Evangelical Leadership Development," *Urban Mission* 12, no. 2 (December 1994): 25-33.

Chapter 1: Capturing the Vision
[1]James P. Spradley, *Participant Observation* (Fort Worth, Tex.: Holt, Rinehart and Winston, 1980), p. 39.
[2]Ibid., pp. vii-viii.

Chapter 2: Who Is My Neighbor?
[1]Barbara Vobejda, "A Diverse U.S. Seen in Census," *Philadelphia Inquirer,* May 30, 1992, pp. A1, A7.
[2]Jerry L. Appleby, *Missions Have Come Home to America: The Church's Cross-cultural Ministry to Ethnics* (Kansas City, Mo.: Beacon Hill, 1986), p. 21.
[3]"The Changing Face of America: How Long Will It Be Before the Third World Overwhelms the First World?" *Time,* July 8, 1985, cover.
[4]"What Will the U.S. Be Like When Whites Are No Longer the Majority?" *Time,* April 9, 1990, cover.
[5]Jorge Taylor, "Equipping Leaders for a Diverse, Multicultural Church," *Theology, News and Notes* 40, no. 4 (December 1993): 11.
[6]David Reimers, "Post-World War II Immigration to the United States: America's Latest Newcomers," *Annals of the American Academy of Political and Social Science* 454 (March 1981): 1.
[7]Robert Pastor, "The Impact of U.S. Immigration Policy on Caribbean Emigra-

tion: Does It Matter?" in *The Caribbean Exodus,* ed. Barry B. Levine (New York: Praeger, 1987), p. 253.

[8]Ibid.

[9]Reimers, "Post-World War II Immigration," p. 7.

[10]Ibid.

[11]Roger Waldinger, "Immigration and Urban Change," *Annual Review of Sociology* 15 (1989): 214.

[12]Ibid., p. 215.

[13]Median family income is a figure indicating that half the families make less, while the other half make more.

Chapter 3: The Purpose of Multiethnic Church Development

[1]C. Peter Wagner, *Leading Your Church to Growth* (Ventura, Calif.: Regal Books, 1984), p. 37.

[2]Luis Centeno, Bethel Temple Community Bible Church, personal communication, September 22, 1994.

[3]Luis Centeno, interview by author, July 13, 1994.

[4]Ibid.

[5]Craig Garriott, phone interview by Sue Baker, Baltimore, Maryland, August 16, 1994.

[6]Ibid.

[7]Ibid.

[8]Ibid.

[9]Ibid.

[10]Ibid.

[11]Michael Walker, interview by author, October 28, 1994.

[12]Ibid.

[13]Craig McMullen, interview by author, August 9, 1994.

[14]Ibid.

[15]Ibid.

[16]Ibid.

[17]S. D. Gaede, *When Tolerance Is No Virtue: Political Correctness, Multiculturalism and the Future of Truth and Justice* (Downers Grove, Ill.: InterVarsity Press, 1993), p. 31.

[18]James Davison Hunter, *Culture Wars: The Struggle to Define America* (New York: HarperCollins, Basic Books, 1991).

[19]David F. Wells, *No Place for Truth, or, Whatever Happened to Evangelical*

Theology? (Grand Rapids, Mich.: Eerdmans, 1993).

[20]Hunter, *Culture Wars,* p. 10.

[21]Ibid.

[22]Os Guinness, *Dining with the Devil: The Megachurch Movement Flirts with Modernity* (Grand Rapids, Mich.: Baker Book House, 1993), p. 78.

Chapter 4: Multicongregational Church Models

[1]C. Peter Wagner, *Church Planting for a Greater Harvest* (Ventura, Calif.: Regal Books, 1990), p. 67.

[2]Jerry Appleby with Glen Van Dyne, *The Church Is in a Stew* (Kansas City, Mo.: Beacon Hill, 1990), p. 18.

[3]Keith Watkins, "Multi-language Congregations: A Field Study in Los Angeles 1993," *Encounter* 55 (Winter 1994): 129-53.

[4]Eleftheria Sidiropoulou, interview by author, August 4, 1994.

[5]Anonymous interview.

[6]Watkins, "Multi-language Congregations," pp. 134-35.

[7]Ibid., p. 135.

[8]Ibid.

[9]Ibid.

[10]Ibid., p. 137.

[11]Ibid.

[12]McKenzie Pier, "First Baptist Church: Heaven's Mirror in Flushing, New York" (final research paper for ME 845, Urban Missions and Evangelism, Seminary of the East, December 18, 1990).

[13]Ibid., p. 1.

[14]Ibid., p. 3.

[15]Ibid., pp. 2-3.

[16]Staff of Flushing First Baptist Church, interview by author, September 28, 1994.

[17]Ibid.

[18]Ibid.

[19]Ibid.

[20]Ibid.

[21]Ibid.

[22]Ibid.

[23]Ibid.

[24]Ibid.

Chapter 5: Multiethnic Church Models

[1]Although we view his church as multiethnic, Kehrein prefers the term *bicultural*, as he makes a distinction between an MEC and a bicultural church. He notes that racial reconciliation between blacks and whites is very complicated. When Hispanics, Asians or others are included, the task is even more complicated and difficult.

[2]S. D. Gaede, *When Tolerance Is No Virtue: Political Correctness, Multiculturalism and the Future of Truth and Justice* (Downers Grove, Ill.: InterVarsity Press, 1993), p. 36.

[3]Ibid., p. 37.

[4]Charles H. Kraft and Marguerite G. Kraft, "Understanding and Valuing Multiethnic Diversity," *Theology, News and Notes* 40, no. 4 (December 1993): 7.

[5]Mark Edward Oh, *Cultural Pluralism and Multiethnic Congregation as a Ministry Model in an Urban Society* (Ann Arbor, Mich.: UMI Dissertation Services, 1988), p. 37.

[6]Ibid., p. 35.

[7]Ibid.

[8]Ibid., p. 36.

[9]Ibid., p. 39.

[10]Ibid., p. 113.

[11]Ibid., p. 114.

[12]Ibid., p. 116.

[13]Ibid., p. 122.

[14]Ibid., p. 123.

[15]Ibid.

[16]Ibid., p. 125.

[17]Ibid.

[18]Kraft and Kraft, "Understanding and Valuing Multiethnic Diversity," p. 7.

[19]Glen Kehrein, interview by author, July 21, 1994.

[20]Ibid.

[21]Ibid.

[22]Ibid.

[23]Ibid.

[24]Raleigh Washington and Glen Kehrein, *Breaking Down Walls* (Chicago: Moody Press, 1993), pp. 116-17.

[25]Ibid., p. 119.

[26]Ibid., p. 126.

[27]Ibid., p. 128.
[28]Ibid., p. 131.
[29]Ibid., p. 170.
[30]Ibid., p. 198.

Chapter 6: Multiethnic Leadership

[1]John Perkins, "May 8 Undergraduate Commencement 1994," *Wheaton Alumni,* Autumn 1994, p. 12.

[2]Ted Ward, "Servants, Leaders and Tyrants," in *Missions and Theological Education in World Perspective,* ed. Harvie M. Conn and Samuel F. Rowen (Farmington, Mich.: Associates of Urbanus, 1984), pp. 19-40. Quoted in Edgar J. Elliston and J. Timothy Kauffman, *Developing Leaders for Urban Ministries* (New York: Peter Lang, 1993), p. 7.

[3]Os Guinness, *Fit Bodies, Fat Minds: Why Evangelicals Don't Think and What to Do About It* (Grand Rapids, Mich.: Baker Book House, 1994), p. 49.

[4]C. René Padilla, "The Unity of the Church and the Homogeneous Unit Principle," in *Exploring Church Growth,* ed. Wilbert R. Shenk (Grand Rapids, Mich.: Eerdmans, 1983), p. 287.

[5]Guinness, *Fit Bodies, Fat Minds.*

[6]Padilla, "The Unity of the Church," p. 288.

Chapter 7: Preparing the Church for Multiethnic Transition

[1]James Westgate, "Transition and the Urban Church," *Urban Mission* 2, no. 4 (March 1985): 22-32.

[2]Ibid.

[3]Craig Ellison, "Attitudes and Urban Transition," *Urban Mission* 2, no. 3 (January 1985): 21.

[4]C. René Padilla, "The Unity of the Church and the Homogeneous Unit Principle," in *Exploring Church Growth,* ed. Wilbert R. Shenk (Grand Rapids, Mich.: Eerdmans, 1983), p. 285.

[5]Charles H. Kraft and Marguerite G. Kraft, "Understanding and Valuing Multiethnic Diversity," *Theology, News and Notes* 40, no. 4 (December 1993): 7.

Chapter 8: Building a New Humanity

[1]Paul G. Hiebert, personal communication, August 12, 1994.

[2]C. René Padilla, "The Unity of the Church and the Homogeneous Unit Principle," in *Exploring Church Growth,* ed. Wilbert R. Shenk (Grand Rapids, Mich.:

Eerdmans, 1983), p. 287.

[3]Mark Edward Oh, *Cultural Pluralism and Multiethnic Congregation as a Ministry Model in an Urban Society* (Ann Arbor, Mich.: UMI Dissertation Services, 1988), p. 138.

[4]Ibid., p. 39.

[5]Ibid., p. 41.

[6]Ibid.

[7]Ibid., p. 43.

[8]Raleigh Washington and Glen Kehrein, *Breaking Down Walls* (Chicago: Moody Press, 1993), pp. 103-11.

[9]Ibid., p. 107.

[10]Ibid., p. 108.

[11]Ibid.

Chapter 9: Do Your Homework!

[1]C. René Padilla, "The Unity of the Church and the Homogeneous Unit Principle," in *Exploring Church Growth,* ed. Wilbert R. Shenk (Grand Rapids, Mich.: Eerdmans, 1983), p. 287, including quote from Donald Guthrie, *Galatians* (London: Thomas Nelson, 1969), p. 115.

Appendix

[1]Paul G. Hiebert, Trinity Evangelical Divinity School, personal communication, August 12, 1994.

[2]Michael Mata, Claremont College, personal communication, August 25, 1994.

[3]Roger Greenway, Calvin Seminary, personal communication, August 25, 1994.

[4]Hoover Wong, Fuller Theological Seminary, personal communication, August 25, 1994.

[5]Robert Lupton, Atlanta, personal communication, August 11, 1994.

Bibliography

Appleby, Jerry L. *Missions Have Come Home to America: The Church's Cross-cultural Ministry to Ethnics.* Kansas City, Mo.: Beacon Hill, 1986.

Appleby, Jerry, with Glen Van Dyne. *The Church Is in a Stew.* Kansas City, Mo.: Beacon Hill, 1990.

Augsburger, David W. *Conflict Mediation Across Cultures: Pathways and Patterns.* Louisville, Ky.: Westminster/John Knox, 1992.

Ellison, Craig. "Attitudes and Urban Transition." *Urban Mission* 2, no. 3 (January 1985): 14-26.

Elliston, Edgar J., and J. Timothy Kauffman. *Developing Leaders for Urban Ministries.* New York: Peter Lang, 1993.

Gaede, S. D. *When Tolerance Is No Virtue: Political Correctness, Multiculturalism and the Future of Truth and Justice.* Downers Grove, Ill.: InterVarsity Press, 1993.

Guinness, Os. *Dining with the Devil: The Megachurch Movement Flirts with Modernity.* Grand Rapids, Mich.: Baker Book House, 1993.

————. *Fit Bodies, Fat Minds: Why Evangelicals Don't Think and What to Do About It.* Grand Rapids, Mich.: Baker Book House, 1994.

Hunter, James Davison. *Culture Wars: The Struggle to Define America.* New York: HarperCollins, Basic Books, 1991.

Kraft, Charles H., and Marguerite G. Kraft. "Understanding and Valuing Multiethnic Diversity." *Theology, News and Notes* 40, no. 4 (December 1993): 6-8.

Oh, Mark Edward. *Cultural Pluralism and Multiethnic Congregation as a Ministry Model in an Urban Society.* Ann Arbor, Mich.: UMI Dissertation Services, 1988.

Padilla, C. René. "The Unity of the Church and the Homogeneous Unit Principle." In *Exploring Church Growth,* edited by Wilbert R. Shenk, pp. 285-303. Grand

Rapids, Mich.: Eerdmans, 1983.

Pastor, Robert. "The Impact of U.S. Immigration Policy on Caribbean Emigration: Does It Matter?" In *The Caribbean Exodus,* edited by Barry B. Levine, pp. 242-59. New York: Praeger, 1987.

Perkins, John M. "May 8 Undergraduate Commencement 1994." *Wheaton Alumni,* Autumn 1994, p. 12.

Pier, McKenzie. "First Baptist Church: Heaven's Mirror in Flushing, New York." Final research paper for ME 845, Urban Missions and Evangelism, Seminary of the East, December 18, 1990.

Reimers, David. "Post-World War II Immigration to the United States: America's Latest Newcomers." *Annals of the American Academy of Political and Social Science* 454 (March 1981): 1-12.

Spradley, James P. *Participant Observation.* Fort Worth, Tex.: Holt, Rinehart and Winston, 1980.

Taylor, Jorge J. "Equipping Leaders for a Diverse, Multicultural Church." *Theology, News and Notes* 40, no. 4 (December 1993): 11-13.

Wagner, C. Peter. *Church Planting for a Greater Harvest.* Ventura, Calif.: Regal Books, 1990.

_____ . *Leading Your Church to Growth.* Ventura, Calif.: Regal Books, 1984.

Waldinger, Roger. "Immigration and Urban Change." *Annual Review of Sociology* 15 (1989): 211-32.

Washington, Raleigh, and Glen Kehrein. *Breaking Down Walls.* Chicago: Moody Press, 1993.

Watkins, Keith. "Multi-language Congregations: A Field Study in Los Angeles 1993." *Encounter* 55 (Winter 1994): 129-53.

Wells, David F. *No Place for Truth, or, Whatever Happened to Evangelical Theology?* Grand Rapids, Mich.: Eerdmans, 1993.

Westgate, James. "Transition and the Urban Church." *Urban Mission* 2, no. 4 (March 1985): 14-26.